THE HOOK BOOK

Jacket illustration. LION, 39 by 67½ inches, hooked by Dorothy Hill. The pattern was specially adapted by Edith Dana from a rug in The American Museum, Bath, England. It is believed that the design was created in upper New York State because of the beavers that appear in the original pattern. The background of the rug shown here was dyed with silver gray over a clear, light blue. The gentle lion was hooked from a tweed jacket that belonged to Mrs. Hill's father and many of the golds were from an old blanket from her mother's trousseau.

THE HOOK BOOK

Alice Beatty and Mary Sargent

with photographs by Lucinda Dowell and
drawings by Barbara Kellogg

Stackpole Books

The Hook Book

Copyright © 1977 by
Alice Beatty and Mary Sargent

Published by
STACKPOLE BOOKS
Cameron and Kelker Streets
P.O. Box 1831
Harrisburg, Pa. 17105

Published simultaneously in Don Mills, Ontario, Canada
by Thomas Nelson & Sons, Ltd.

Printed in the U.S.A.

Library of Congress Cataloging in Publication Data

Beatty, Alice, 1902-
    The hook book.

    1. Rugs, Hooked.   I. Sargent, Mary Clary, joint
author.   II. Title.
TT850.B33 1977   746.7'4   77-5852
ISBN 0-8117-0820-9

To Stella Hay Rex
Who Has Inspired Many
to Hook Primitive Rugs

CONTENTS

INTRODUCTION

As one of Alice Beatty's students for more than a decade, I was continually awed by her knowledge of primitive hooking, her innate sense of color and texture, and her talent for helping hundreds of students to produce handsome rugs, every one an individual work of art, unlike any other. Though she has taught for twenty-five years, her enthusiasm has never waned, and she calls the rugs created in her studio her "children."

As an outstanding authority on hooking primitive rugs, Alice Beatty has played a leading role in perpetuating this craft. The American Folk Art Museum recognized the craft as an Early American art form when it mounted an exhibition in New York in 1974. Record attendance at this function was witness of the new interest generated.

As my own interest in hooking grew, I became obsessed with the idea that Alice Beatty's knowledge and inspiration should be captured as a permanent record, so that many more craftsmen could benefit from her experience. I convinced her that we had the makings of a perfect collaboration, with her expertise in teaching and in hooking primitive rugs and my profession as a writer whose hobby is hooking.

The Hook Book reflects the talents of many persons. We are indebted to Lucinda Dowell, photographer, and Barbara Kellogg, artist, for their personal interest in providing the best possible photographs and line drawings for the book. We should also like to thank all those who were kind enough to lend their rugs to be photographed and the designers whose patterns were used. These artists make a large contribution to this craft in providing a wide variety of beautiful designs for rugmaking.

We hope that *The Hook Book* will spark your interest in hooking primitive rugs and that you will find in the craft the same joy that so many others have found, from the American pioneers to your contemporaries.

Mary Sargent

CHAPTER 1

You and Rug Hooking

Primitive crafts, once doomed to machine-age oblivion, are enjoying a lively revival. They are a favorite pastime of those who refuse to be gobbled up by an electronic age that quashes individuality. Everybody has a born desire to create. And to make something with your own hands is a form of self-expression and relaxation that soothed even the caveman after a hard day on the prowl. Today, this kind of creativeness offers not only fulfillment of the artist-ego but also a line of defense against a programmed life of push buttons and plastic.

Craftily Creative

Studios have sprung up coast to coast in basements, churches, boutiques, and classrooms, where eager artisans ply crafts, such as leaded-glass, macramé, and leather work. These little groups have discovered with glee what hands can do—especially their own! And there is no brighter glint in the eye than that of a craftsman who is wielding a small hook over a rug in progress. In the words of George A. Dorr, Jr., president of Dorr Woolen Company, which manufactures fine wool fabrics for rugmaking, "Hooking rugs can be the ultimate in creativity. You can design your own patterns, dye your colors, cut wool strips by hand, and hook them into a foundation to make a beautiful rug."

The origin of hooking has not been established conclusively, but we have documentation that fabrics were hooked in Egypt as far back as the fifth century. And displayed in the Oslo Museum of Norway are examples of hooking made by the Vikings. Although this skill was brought to the Colonies from Europe, it soon became a distinctly American folk art. The pioneers practiced the old New England proverb "Use it up, wear it out, make it do, or do without" by hooking bits and pieces of wool into foundation fabrics to make bed and floor coverings. The lives of articles of clothing, sometimes more difficult to acquire than food and shelter, could be extended in this way. Through their Yankee thrift, the early American settlers brought beauty into their homes as well. Craftsmen today use the same technique as that of the pioneers, though modern equipment surpasses the crude tools originally used. Rugs created in this manner are called primitives.

Primitive Hooking for Today's Craftsmen

"Primitive hooking" refers to the manner in which a rug is hooked as well as to the appearance of the final product. Strips of wool fabric, not yarn, form the loops and make a thick, sturdy rug. Combinations of both coarse and fine textures give depth and character to the rug. Primitive rugs resemble primitive American paintings. Patterns are usually simple outlines in bold design, sometimes childlike, with little attention to scale or perspective. In one charming traditional pattern, the flowers grow taller than the house beside them.

Many rugs hooked today are copies or adaptations of nineteenth-century rugs. These primitives, in their sheer simplicity, lend warmth and interest to any room in a home, whether traditional or modern in decor. Colors may be muted and mellow to blend with antiques or splashy and bright to accent contemporary surroundings.

Primitive rugs are not to be confused with a kind of hooked rug called "realistic"; although the same basic technique is used for both, the rugs produced are very different. Realistic patterns are more delicate and formal, conveying a photographic realism, in contrast to primitives, which are bolder and more dramatic. For realistic hooking the wool strips are cut as fine as yarn, and a certain beauty of texture is lost.

You Too Can Make a Rug

Almost anybody can make a rug in the same way as the American pioneers did. A dearth of dexterity is no deterrent. If you're "all thumbs," those thumbs will help you hook. Even a beginner finds instant pleasure in this craft, once the simple routine of using a hook is mastered. Within minutes you sense the joy of creating, as a leaf or a strawberry takes shape before your eyes. And rare is the person who isn't hooked on hooking after completing a first rug. One woman learned to hook for the purely practical purpose of making one area rug to cover a worn spot in her broadloom carpet. Now, twenty-seven rugs later, she still anticipates the next—and the next—and the next. And at least a half-dozen of her friends have caught the same fever.

Since the name of the craft is hooking, be prepared for a lot of good-natured ribbing—and a few raised eyebrows! On one occasion, a few eager beginners, on their separate ways to a first hooking lesson and unfamiliar with the location of the studio, happened to stop and ask the same policeman for direc-

13

tions. By the third inquiry, the officer became curious and asked the young woman what was going on there. She cheerfully answered, ''A beginning class for hookers,'' and drove on. The class had barely begun when the officer appeared at the door to investigate. At the sight of eight ladies bending over frames with little hooks in their hands, he hastily retreated, apologizing profusely.

Hook a Little Fun Into Your Life

Rugmaking is a hobby for everyone:

- The young, who crave freedom of expression.

- The old, who have hung up their skis in favor of more sedentary sports.

- The busy mother, harried and housebound, in need of diversion. One mother holds court at her rug frame from eight to nine a.m. daily, when she hooks out family frustrations, along with her own. As her children present problems, she untangles hair and arbitrates arguments between loops.

- The lonely and the shut-ins, whose time hangs heavy. The rug you hook will be a magic carpet that makes empty hours take flight.

- The business woman with little leisure. Since you can start or stop hooking at any point, without confusion, this hobby can be

14

squeezed into the tightest schedule. Hook a stem in the time it takes to perk a pot of morning coffee. Top it with a flower as you wind down at the end of the day.

- A retired man who is casting about for new interests. Yes, men *do* hook; it has often been a pastime of seafaring men. One teen-ager, six feet tall and all rugged male, borrowed his mother's rug frame and designed and hooked his own rug.

- The live-in grandmother, who needs interests and activities of her own.

- The extrovert. Group hooking is ideal for people who need people. Total concentration is rarely necessary, so it's a hook-and-chatter hobby that encourages friendships. Some groups meet for all-day hooking bees with time out for lunches and coffee breaks.

- The introvert. People who don't need people like hooking too. It's a hobby you can pursue just as easily alone.

- The incapacitated, whose physical limitations exclude many activities. One heart patient, who might otherwise have been destined for a life of inactivity and boredom, has created an enviable display of handsome rugs. Even those with impaired sight can hook, because there is little eye strain. Once the motion of using the hook becomes automatic, much of the work is done through the sense of touch.

15

Practical Pleasure

One of the more obvious reasons for hooking, not to be overlooked by the hobby-happy, is the permanent pleasure of possessing one-of-a-kind rugs that add distinction to a home, as they mellow into heirlooms of the future. There is no more practical hobby. What other way do you know to acquire priceless treasures of museum quality by using the contents of a ragbag and your outmoded clothing? As a lagniappe, you make a patriotic contribution to ecology by recycling wool. Many rugs can be hooked without any purchase of even the most inexpensive new wool.

Yours to Enjoy Forever

Hooked rugs will outlast most other floor coverings. You need never flinch when family and friends tramp over your favorites. These rugs are not fragile decorations to be hung on a wall or carefully avoided when you cross a room. Use actually heightens their beauty. Some teachers prefer that rugs for exhibit be at least two years old, rather than fresh off a frame. One beginner, impatient for her first success to appear as an heirloom, gave a wall-to-wall cocktail party with the hope that a hundred pairs of shoes would promote instant aging of her rug.

A hooking buff can rarely subdue his enthusiasm once aroused, and continues to hook for one room after another—from living room to kitchen, up the stairway, into bedrooms and even baths. Although many rugmakers hook room-sized rugs, area or scatter rugs are the most popular and combine well with commercially-made broadlooms. Area rugs add interest when placed at random on a solid-color carpet: in front of a hearth, under a coffee table, in an entrance hall, or beside a bed.

If you eventually run out of floor space, there's no need to lay aside your hook. Make a set of hooked chair seats or a cover for footstool or bench. You can even go "pro"; there's money to be made if you can bear to part with something that has so much soul hooked in. Most craftsmen, of course, would sooner sell their children than their rugs! But a handmade rug is an incomparable gift of love to someone you cherish.

CHAPTER 2

From Rags to Rug Riches

If you have the heart of a collector, you are blessed with the instincts of a true rugger, because collecting and hoarding wool fabrics to insure a continuous supply go hand in hand with hooking. And the greater the variety of textures in your collection, the more beautiful your rugs will be.

By badgering friends and family, you can build an impressive cache of wool to dip into whenever needed. Friends soon learn that the hungry look in your eye means you covet their clothes for a rug. But once they see the miracles performed with a hook, they will take pride in having their garments converted into a permanent remembrance of clothing once worn. Thus, a rug becomes a sentimental collage of family and friendships.

Be wise and greedily grab all the wool you can lay your hands on, early in your career as a rugmaker. Later, as your friends become inspired by your rugs, they will use their discarded garments for their *own* rugs, and you will have to find other sources. Don't be timid about spreading the word among chance acquaintances. Sometimes people you have barely met become your most bounteous providers and turn up with windfalls of woolens. They are delighted to find a convenient outlet for scraps from sewing and the overflow from attics. Blessed are the givers!

Graciously accept anything (yes, anything!) offered, whether or not you can use it, so that you won't alienate wool-bearing friends. If you decline fabrics or make an issue of what you can and can't use, friends may become discouraged and lose interest in your project. You can always turn over your rejects to a favorite charity.

Woolgathering

There are a few guidelines to follow when collecting woolens. A rug is only as good as the material you hook into it. Fabric that is 100 percent wool is categorically the very best material for hooking, superior to cottons and synthetics, because of its durability, resistance to soiling, and dyeing qualities. It's better to buy all new wool by the yard, even if you have to overdye it, than to compromise by using fabrics made of a wool and synthetic combination just because you have them on hand. Although many of these combinations are flooding the market, you can still find enough pure wool if you set your mind to it. (See Appendix.)

Although the best rule is never to use anything but pure wool in a rug, there is one possible exception. You may use a wool-synthetic combination *if it need not be dyed.* Synthetic fabrics do not absorb dye in the same way as wool, and boiling can affect their wearing quality. Fabrics containing synthetics should be used only in very small quantities, as accents, such as outlines or flower stems and centers. Don't be lured into using these fabrics in large quantities, no matter how pretty they are.

Look for labels in garments or on bolts of wool that indicate whether or not they are pure wool. If you don't know the fiber content of a fabric, give it the match test. Pull two threads, one from each direction, so that you have both warp and woof. Or pull any thread that looks different from others. Hold a lighted match first to one thread and then to the other. A wool thread will emit an odor of burning hair or feathers. A cotton thread will burn quickly with little or no odor. A synthetic thread burns with no odor.

Although fabrics of medium weight are easiest to handle, you will need a variety of weights for interesting effects. Firmly-woven fabrics, especially flannels and tightly-woven medium-weight tweeds, are the best for a beginner to work with, because they can be pulled through the foundation without effort and without raveling. A loose weave that ravels is difficult to handle. A more experienced worker can cope with it by cutting wider strips and hooking carefully so that threads aren't separated or pulled apart. Reserve your loose weaves for a second rug when you have become an expert. Some wool blankets are suitable for hooking, but very heavy blankets are not easy to work with, especially for a beginner; if you use them at all, cut strips *very* narrow. Navy blankets that are almost like felt are totally unsuitable. And by all means reject blankets with cotton or synthetic fibers running one way; these threads do not absorb dye well, soil easily, and can't be cleaned well.

Wool to Have and to Hook

To provide a variety of textures, try to have as many different kinds of wool on hand as possible. Here are some to look for:

> solid colors
> plaids
> herringbones
> checks
> stripes
> heather effects
> paisley patterns (old paisley shawls that are damaged may sometimes be found in thrift shops at bargain prices)
> wool crepes (use only in small quantities, for accents)
> mohair (use sparingly, for occasional variation in texture)

Unsuitable for Hooking

Avoid using the following fabrics; the texture is either too hard, too stretchy, or too delicate:

> gabardine
> serge
> jersey and all other knitted fabrics
> all worsteds
> diagonal weaves (they fray when cut in strips)
> cashmere (doesn't wear well but could be used in *very small quantities*)

Wool of almost any color is useable, because it can be overdyed or bleached and redyed. Of course, light colors and pastels are more easily altered. Commercially-dyed blacks, browns, and navy blues are usually too harsh in color, unless they are to be used as sharp contrasts to carry out a very modern decorating theme, such as sharp black against white. Though they can be treated to take on softer effects, commercial blacks, browns and navies are avoided by most rugmakers, who prefer to dye their own (see page 88).

Your Scavenger Hunt

It sometimes becomes a challenge to ferret out just the right fabrics needed, but there are many sources where you can find suitable woolens for a moderate amount of money, or indeed free for the asking. And whatever remains from one rug can be used in others.

21

EARLY RAILROAD, 36 by 75 inches, Craftsman pattern No. H152, hooked by Judith Ann Truedson. This New England scene is for an experienced rugmaker. Light gray wool, overdyed in very light chartreuse, makes an interesting sky. Different textures and values are hooked in horizontal rows. The wool for the road was bright red, boiled out and overdyed in a small quantity of seal brown. Roundhouse is red-and-brown checks.

Here are some of the favorite haunts of rugmakers:

- Shops and mail order houses that feature new rug woolens by the yard or by the pound, and remnants, seconds, or mill ends, at reasonable prices. Excellent sources for backgrounds and other large areas that require large quantities.

- Thrift shops where secondhand clothing is sold. They sometimes *give away* garments that are torn or moth-eaten, so always ask about these.

- Rummage sales. Volunteer to help and you'll have first choice.

- Salvation Army shops where secondhand clothes are sold.

And don't overlook the possibilities in wool scraps from sewing and alterations, such as strips from shortened skirts, dresses, and pants. Ask your tailor for his scraps.

Care of Woolens Before Storing

There's nothing like cleanliness to keep a moth at bay, and detergents are double trouble to the moth world. Woolens can be safely stored for years, without a single moth-bite, if washed with detergent in warm water (either by hand or machine), rinsed, and thoroughly dried. Treat all woolens in this way, including brand-new fabrics and freshly dry-cleaned garments, and especially your secondhand bargains from thrift shops. Besides discouraging moths, washing has other advantages for the rugmaker. It removes any filler or cleaning fluid, softens the wool, and tightens the weave.

Before storing, dismantle all garments. First remove linings, interlinings, and shoulder pads; then, wash and dry the garment before further dismantling. After it is washed, pull open the seams; a vigorous tug will usually do it. If not, don't waste time ripping stitches; just cut along the seams. Also cut around buttonholes, pockets, and zippers, and cut off skirt bands. Open sleeve seams. Cut out worn areas. Discard the thin, shiny seats of pants in favor of the sturdy legs.

When all the seams of one garment have been ripped or cut open, lay the pieces flat, one on top of another. Then roll into a tight bundle and tie securely. If you keep like woolens together in one bundle, you will always know how much of any one fabric you have. And as your backlog of wool builds, you will avoid having to search through mounds of fabric for matching pieces. When you have only a few pieces of one fabric, simply pin them together with a large safety pin.

It's wise to keep samples of each fabric, about six by fifteen inches, on a big safety pin or shower-curtain ring, so that you can quickly see what you have on hand.

Keep bundles of wool in large clear plastic bags so that you can spot colors readily. As an added safeguard against moths, toss in a few moth balls. Since these bags are light and flexible, they can be easily transported when you work with a group in other homes or studios. Avoid leaving plastic bags in the sun; moisture can collect within the bags and cause the wool to mildew, or your colors may fade.

Some rugmakers prefer to group their wools by color, while others combine similar weights and textures. Work out whatever system pleases you. However, you will find it helpful to have all plaids, checks and stripes together in one bag. Also, keep one separate bag for very small odds and ends that may be just enough for a stem, a bud, or a cat's tail. There's always a spot for the tiniest bit of wool, so never throw anything away recklessly.

Hooking doesn't require a lot of regimentation that spoils all the fun. Of course, those with a fetish for order can organize to their hearts' content, but the most disorganized workers muddle through with equally handsome rugs. A little organization does help, though, in facilitating work and keeping a tidier workroom.

CHAPTER 3

Choosing a Pattern and Color Planning

Almost any kind of design that appeals to you in other forms of decoration can be adapted to hooked rugs—flowers, fruits, animals, birds, scenes, geometrics, scrolls, and simple stripes. Hobbies, such as boating or fishing, can inspire designs. Early-day craftsmen simply sketched their favorite things —valentines, weather vanes, glass and china patterns, hex signs, houses, barns, quilt patterns, even the family pet—onto foundation fabrics.

It's best to select a small size for your first rug. By completing it within a reasonably short time, you gain confidence and a desire to create more rugs. And you can learn a lot about hooking from one small rug. Three patterns, suitable for beginners, are described in detail in Chapter 13.

Commercially Stenciled Patterns

The name Edward Sands Frost means patterns to those who hook rugs. Around 1868 he became the very first person to make and sell patterns commercially in this country. Beginning as a tin peddler, traveling around New England, he became interested in his customers' rugmaking but deplored the dearth of good design. With an "I-can-do-it-better" spirit, he created a supply of metal stencils made from old wash boilers, so that he could stencil his own patterns on burlap and sell them in quantity. Skeptics laughed at this endeavor, predicting that it would never last, but the new business flourished. Though his ingenuity discouraged his customers' creativity, it did stimulate interest and enthusiasm in hooking.

PRINCE, 26 by 38 inches, Edana pattern No. 46, hooked by Evelyn Urciuoli. This prancing horse is a copy of an original Frost pattern. Background is gray-blue commercially-dyed new wool. The wreath is a series of small scrolls, each hooked in red on one side and in gray and red plaid on the other. The same plaid is used in corner leaves.

In the 1930's, Ralph Burnham of Ipswich, Massachusetts, became the catalyst for renewed interest in hooking. Mr. Burnham, already a celebrated collector, started rescuing antique rugs that were doomed to oblivion, thus preserving a part of this country's heritage. He reproduced these old patterns on burlap and offered them for sale. After Ralph Burnham's death, Mrs. Carl Hall of Rye, New Hampshire, purchased the Burnham patterns from his wife. They are now available from Joan Moshimer (see Appendix).

Today, more than a century after Edward Sands Frost produced the first commercial designs, hundreds of handsome patterns, stenciled on burlap or monk's cloth, are available at modest prices from purveyors of rugmaking equipment, or directly from artists who specialize in designing and stenciling rugs. Catalogs can usually be ordered for small sums. Occasionally patterns of rugs are offered for sale through magazines that feature them in special articles. The rugs pictured in this book may be ordered from the suppliers named if you specify the name of the rug and the order number (see Appendix).

Something for Everyone

There are adaptations of traditional patterns to please antique buffs, many in the folk-art tradition, patterns that are clearly contemporary, and patterns with an oriental flavor. In their simplicity, many nineteenth-century designs look surprisingly modern when hooked in vibrant twentieth-century colors.

Rugs are never boring look-alikes when hooked in different colors and different fabrics, even when identical patterns are used. In one California home that features the last word in contemporary design, the highlight of the decor is a rug hooked in sunny yellows and burnt orange. Though it passes for to-day's design, the original pattern was created in 1825. The same pattern, hooked in muted colors by a woman in New Jersey, appropriately comple-ments a home filled with antiques.

The Shape of Rugs to Come

The place where a rug is to be used will determine your choice of size, shape and design. There are rounds, half-rounds, squares, oblongs, ovals, and long, narrow rugs for stairs and halls. Select a pattern that is a suitable size to begin with. If you attempt to alter the size to suit your space, you will probably dis-tort a well-balanced design.

Many patterns, such as those featuring scenes or animals, are one-way designs, best viewed from one direction. These rugs can provide interest in many areas of a home—beside a bed, in an alcove, or before a fireplace, bu-reau, or sink. A one-way design may also be placed at the foot or head of a stairway. Study the directions from which a rug will be seen when you select a pattern.

Your Own Originals

Sooner or later, you may feel the urge to design a rug yourself. With only a flair for sketching and an idea, you can have the fun of creating an original pattern without qualifying as a skilled artist. If you can't draw, you can hook bands of colors in hit-or-miss fashion and still make a rug that is yours alone.

Incidentally, this is an ideal way to use up odds and ends of all kinds of fabrics.

Colonial women, without formal training, created designs that have become classics, with only the aid of homely devices, such as dinner plates as patterns for circular designs, and half-burned sticks to make charcoal tracings. Yet many of their rugs are now the pride of fine museums.

Whenever you see rugs you like, make notes and sketches for future reference. Clip pictures of rugs featured in magazine articles. Study rugs in museums. Fabrics and wallpapers may provide inspiration. Since realism is not important in primitive rugs, it matters little whether the species of a flower can be identified, as long as it's plainly a flower. Often the charm of a design is its very incongruity. In one popular pattern, adapted from a nineteenth-century rug, smoke from a chimney drifts in one direction, while a flag flutters in the opposite direction. Nobody cares which way the wind blows! (See Color Plate No. 1.) Another appealing design features a big cat, twice the size of the house beside it. (See Color Plate No. 2.)

Drawings by children are often a source of inspiration for hooked rugs. (See Color Plate No. 3.) Their simple honesty and direct approach is an ideal technique for designing primitive rugs. Without hesitation or apology, children draw bold lines to represent sunshine or giant flowers growing from a tiny pot. One woman translates her children's drawings into rugs for their rooms. Look to the future, though, when hooking for children; a pattern that delights youngsters may be scorned as they reach their teens. (Then the juvenile rug may become a hand-me-down for a younger brother or sister.) There are many subjects, however—animals, cottages, boats—that are suitable for a child's room, yet will be treasured a lifetime.

When drawing your own pattern, give attention to the following:

Composition. The eye should be drawn to the center of the rug.

Simplicity. Strive for an uncluttered look and avoid delicate details that are unsuitable for primitive rugs.

Balance. Although primitives do not require perfect balance, the area of design at one side or end of a rug should not outweigh the design at the opposite side or end. And there should be a comparable area of background at each end.

Rug Foundations

The foundation of a rug may be of either burlap, available in 38- to 48-inch width, or of monk's cloth. Meriwell Rug Backing, an excellent cotton monk's cloth, is available in 54-, 92-, and 184-inch widths (see Appendix). Preference is purely personal. Some designers believe that monk's cloth will outwear burlap—but burlap will usually last a lifetime. And while some rugmakers find burlap easier to work on, because it provides a firmer surface, others are equally enthusiastic over monk's cloth because of its soft quality. (A beginner may find the firm surface of burlap easier to learn on.)

If you prefer burlap, purchase either eight-and-one-half-ounce Scotch burlap or ten-ounce burlap from India. And insist on one of these burlaps when ordering stenciled patterns. This is one time that top quality with tight weave is not advantageous, because it cannot accommodate the wide strips of wool or the type of hook used in primitives. The less expensive burlap has a more open weave that is better for this kind of hooking. Before purchasing burlap by the yard, check for flaws by holding it to the light. If there are breaks in the fibers, do not buy it, because holes will appear in your rug wherever fibers are broken.

From the Glint in Your Eye to a Finished Pattern

These suggestions will help you to construct your pattern.

Draw the outline of your rug on the foundation, using a black or dark blue felt marker, to establish the size and shape. Make sure that the outline is straight on the burlap or monk's cloth. All corners should be perfect right angles, and rounds should be perfectly round. Measure accurately with a yardstick as a guide when drawing straight border lines.

Leave generous margins of foundation on all sides, at least three or four inches beyond the outline of the rug, so that there will be adequate space for attaching it to the frame and for turning a hem when the rug is completed.

After you have decided on the kind of design you wish to make—whether flowers, scrolls, leaves, stars, or animals—cut patterns of coarse sandpaper or cardboard. (Sandpaper patterns won't slip when you trace them.) Experiment with composition by moving the patterns around on the foundation until you find the best arrangement.

There are two ways to transfer a design to the foundation of a rug after making a drawing of the pattern in the actual size intended: (1) Transfer pencils have become a boon to the arts and crafts set. After you draw your pattern on transparent tracing paper, simply trace the pattern with the pencil. Place pattern, pencil-side down, against the foundation, and go over it with a hot iron to transfer it to the foundation. You can prevent reversing the design by following the lines of the pattern with the transfer pencil on the *wrong* side of the paper. Do not use heavy paper; heat cannot sufficiently penetrate to make clear lines on the foundation. The Joan Moshimer Pattern Pencil may be ordered from W. Cushing & Company (See Appendix). The Vogart pencil is available in arts and crafts shops.

(2) An alternate method of constructing a pattern is to draw it on any kind of paper (you can use brown wrapping paper) and then transfer it to net. Place the net over your drawing, and, with a felt marker, trace the design onto the net. To transfer the design from net to foundation, lay the net pattern over the foundation, checking to make sure that the design is straight. Pin net and foundation together on all sides. With felt marker, again trace the design, following the lines of the net pattern. The ink will go through the open mesh, leaving a clear pattern on the foundation after the net is removed. (Net can be purchased by the yard where sewing supplies are sold. It comes as wide as seventy-two inches and is very inexpensive.)

Personally Yours

When a rug is made to celebrate a special occasion, such as a wedding or anniversary, it's nice to hook your initials and the date into it as a permanent reminder. You may wish to date your first rug in this way to establish the year you began your hobby. Some crafty craftsmen like to sneak obscure initials into the design, just as the Old Masters sometimes painted their own faces into crowd scenes.

Color It Right

One of the joys of hooking rugs and dyeing your own colors is that you can have exactly what you like, without compromising. As used in this book, the term *color* refers to hue, such as red or green. *Value* means the degree of lightness or darkness of color. The many grays between black and white are the different values. Pink is one value of red.

The beauty of a hooked rug lies in its color and texture. Since the eye travels color, rather than pattern, a rug is pleasing to the eye when colors and values are well planned, even if design and workmanship lack perfection. So think COLOR, think VALUE, and think TEXTURE. You can learn a lot about combining colors from books on decorating and by studying wallpaper and fabric designs created by professionals.

Avoid great contrasts in values throughout a rug. The most striking contrast should be that between pattern and background, with pattern predominating against a quiet background. Changes in value should be gradual within areas of design to prevent spottiness. It's usually best to avoid very bright colors, except as accents in small quantities, such as a row or two of outlining. Most bright colors are more pleasing when softened or dulled.

Choose the color for the background of a rug first, because that will chart the course of colors and values to be selected for the pattern. And each color within the design must look right against the background. When planning a background, think about the rug's location and the traffic there. Since very

SQUARE RIGGER, 30½ by 44 inches, Heritage Hill pattern No. 44A, hooked by Joanna Orton. The effect of white sails against a deep blue background is striking. Medium gray wool was overdyed in sky blue. A touch of white was subtly brought into the border by sandwiching it between two rows of red.

light backgrounds show soil quickly in a kitchen or entrance hall, dark backgrounds are more practical for these areas. Strong colors hold up best where a rug is exposed to lots of sunshine. And light colors can brighten the dark corners of a home.

Black makes a rich-looking background, but blacks that you dye yourself will look softer and warmer than those commercially dyed. Many handsome backgrounds that appear black actually have very little true black in them. They are made of different colors and textures of wool, dyed together to produce blue-blacks, green-blacks, brown-blacks, and gray-blacks. When these are hooked together, along with a little pure black, the background becomes mottled and mellow. These dyed blacks are most effective when red plaids and tweeds are overdyed and combined with the other dyed fabrics. Flecks of red continue to peep through even after dyeing, and when sprinkled through the background, they bring life and depth to the black. (See page 88 for dyeing antique black.)

A brown background looks softer and richer if you begin with gray wool and dye it brown, or overdye brown with a weak solution of black dye. If you *do* use commercially-dyed blacks and browns, first lighten or fade them (see page 73).

When you first begin to hook, you can collect enough wool for a dark background more quickly than for a light background, unless you have a lot of light-color fabrics on hand or are willing to purchase them by the yard. Almost any wool fabric can be included in a dark background, because it can be overdyed—and the greater the variety, the better.

As soon as you decide on a color for the background, estimate the quantity of wool that you will need (see Chapter 8), and dye that wool first.

Color It Simple

The pattern of a rug is hooked in medium to light colors on dark backgrounds and in medium to dark colors on light backgrounds. Don't try to include every color you like in one rug, because it will look too busy. It is best to confine colors of a small rug to three, such as red, blue and gold, with one color dominating two supporting colors. And when you select your colors, decide whether you prefer blue-reds or yellow-reds, blue-greens or yellow-greens— the family of colors that appeals to you.

Choose the dominant color first, and carry it throughout the rug, repeating it in outlines, border, and other details, as well as in the main portion of the pattern. Let supporting colors be muted. If red is your leading color, soft gold, instead of bright yellow, is a more pleasing complement. If yellow is the leading color, use soft red, instead of bright red, as a supporting color. For variety, use different textures and different values of the same colors, along with muted tones of gray, khaki, beige or brown.

After you plan colors for the pattern, dye some wool in those colors (see Chapters 8 and 9). Then experiment with arrangements and balance by placing the wool on the pattern, on the floor. Florals are most pleasing when colors are balanced diagonally. For example, an area of rust in the upper left-hand corner should balance with an area of rust in the lower righthand corner. Colors in one-way designs can be balanced left and right. (After your pattern is on the frame, you can always collapse the frame to lie flat on the floor when you want to see how various colors will look.)

You may change some of your ideas when you begin to hook and the design takes shape. It is easier to plan colors and values after some of the wool is hooked into the foundation. Even the most experienced rugmakers let color schemes grow gradually. Trial and error—hooking in colors and pulling out whatever looks wrong—is the best system.

CHAPTER 4

A Smooth Binding Makes a Good Beginning

When a rug is bound correctly, it will always lie flat on the floor, without cupping at the edges. Use cotton twill tape that comes one-and-one-quarter to two inches wide and is made for binding rugs. It can usually be purchased locally from needlework and sewing shops. Do not use adhesive "iron-on" tape. Select the color nearest that planned for the border of the rug or nearest the color of the floor on which the rug will be laid. When you purchase your tape, add an extra few inches to the total measurement of the four sides or the circumference of the rug to avoid running short.

Your Personal Touch

It's nice to embroider your name and date on the binding of a rug before it is sewn to the foundation. Or sew a personalized label onto the binding after the rug is completed. Labels inscribed "Handmade by *(name)*" are often advertised by mail-order houses in magazines and newspapers. When your rug is handed down to posterity—or lands in a museum one hundred years hence—you'll receive credit due.

How to Begin

Tape binding is sewn on the foundation of a rug before you mount the pattern on the frame, but you cannot complete the binding until after the rug has been hooked and removed from the frame. However, the entire procedure is outlined here, so that you will understand it from beginning to end.

Before sewing the tape on, turn under any raw edges of the foundation (selvage edges need not be hemmed), and stitch them either by machine or by hand to prevent raveling. Most stenciled patterns come with edges already hemmed. Lay the tape on the right side of the pattern, not on the margin, *in-side* the outline of the rug itself. Begin and end the binding in the center of one side, never at a corner. Turn back three-fourths-inch at the end of the tape to lap over the other end when the two ends meet. Be sure to follow the outline of the rug with the tape, instead of following a thread in the foundation.

With heavy duty cotton thread, sew the tape by hand. Make very small straight running stitches, about one-eighth-inch long, as close as possible to the edge of the tape (see Fig. 1). Do not stitch the tape by machine, because it tends to pull the edges too tight.

Every few stitches, make a backstitch. It helps to pin a few inches ahead, but don't pin the tape around the entire pattern. It is better to ease it along as you sew. If you hold the foundation and tape across your knee in a slightly curved position as you work, you will avoid pulling it too tight. When you reach a corner, ease the tape around the corner and make a backstitch in the very corner. Do not make tucks in the tape at corners.

How to End

When you have bound all sides, cut off any excess tape, but leave three-fourths-inch to lap over the end that was folded back. When the tape is eventually turned to the other side of the rug, the raw edge will be under the folded end. Do not sew together the two ends until after the rug is hooked and

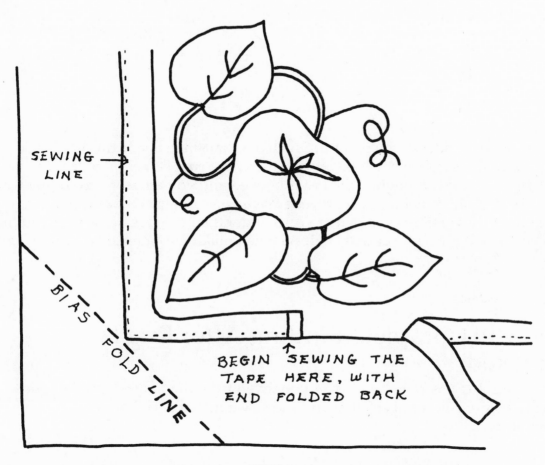

SEWING
LINE

BIAS FOLD LINE

BEGIN SEWING THE
TAPE HERE, WITH
END FOLDED BACK

FIGURE 1

the binding is turned back to be sewn in place. No further sewing is done at this time on the binding.

If you have a sewing machine that can make zigzag stitching, you can avoid extra work when you are ready to hem the foundation later. After the tape binding is sewn to the foundation, and before the pattern is mounted on the frame, lay the pattern, right side up, on a table or floor, with binding out flat on the margin. Draw a line on the margin with a felt marker, the width of the tape, along all sides of the pattern. Stitch one-half-inch inside this line, making continuous zigzag stitching around the entire rug. *Do not cut or trim the margin at this time.* But when the rug is hooked and you are ready to complete the binding, this stitching will prevent raveling as you trim the surplus margin. It also eliminates having to turn under the raw edge of the foundation as you hem it. This is especially helpful when making room-size, round, or oval rugs.

How to Complete Binding After Rug Is Hooked

After your rug has been hooked and removed from the frame, hem the foundation before you turn back the tape and sew it in place. Follow this procedure:

(1)   Unless you have edged the foundation with zigzag stitching, as described above, lay the rug flat on the floor or table, with right side up and tape binding lying out flat on the margin of the foundation. With felt marker, draw a line on the margin of the foundation, along the outer edge of the tape binding to form a cutting line.

(2)   Trim the surplus margin along the cutting line, but cut and hem no more than twelve inches at one time to prevent excessive raveling.

(3)   Fold the remaining margin to the underneath side of the rug. Insert a few pins to hold it in place until it is sewn. Hem it to the wrong side of the rug

with heavy duty cotton thread, turning under raw edges at least one-fourth-inch.(If you have made zigzag stitching, it is unnecessary to turn under raw edges.) Overcast the hem with stitches about one-half-inch apart. Do not pull stitches tight. And make sure that they do not go through to the right side of the rug. The tape is not sewn in place until after the foundation is completely hemmed.

(4) When you reach a corner and have trimmed the margin of the foundation to the correct width, make a true bias fold, straight across the corner of the remaining margin (see Fig. 2). Fold the corner to the underneath side of the rug. Crease or pin the fold line.

(5) Overcast with short stitches along the fold. Trim the excess corner of foundation, about one-fourth-inch away from the overcast fold.

(6) With the corner as the center point, bring together the two halves of the overcast bias edge to form a perfect mitered corner on the underneath side of the rug. Do not sew the two edges of the miter together.

(7) Continue hemming the foundation, mitering each corner, until the hem is completed.

Now you are ready to sew the tape binding in place. After the foundation is hemmed, the tape binding can be easily turned under and sewn to the rug. Overcast with stitches about one-half-inch apart. Again, be sure that stitches cannot be seen on the right side.

When you reach a corner, sew as far as you can to the very end of the side you are working on. When the tape from the side adjoining that corner is folded over it, a mitered corner is automatically formed. *Do not cut off any tape at the corner.* Make a few stitches along the miter to hold it together.

Where the two ends of the tape meet, the end that was folded over at the

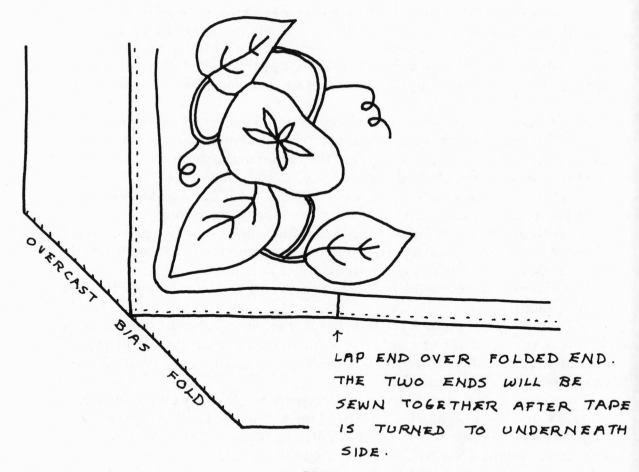

OVERCAST BIAS FOLD

LAP END OVER FOLDED END.
THE TWO ENDS WILL BE
SEWN TOGETHER AFTER TAPE
IS TURNED TO UNDERNEATH
SIDE.

FIGURE 2

beginning is lapped over the end with the raw edge and the two ends are sewn together.

Binding Round or Oval Rugs

Binding round or oval rugs is a little more difficult than binding straight edges. There is no problem when you sew the tape on at the beginning. But when you hem the foundation after the rug is hooked, you have to ease the excess material, caused by the curve, into the hem and make it as smooth as possible. This is when zigzag stitching on the foundation really helps. (See page 41.) The tape can be slightly shirred with a straight, running stitch just before it is turned back to be sewn in place. This makes it easier to distribute the surplus evenly along the curves.

CHAPTER 5

Frames for Hooking and How to Use Them

In any endeavor, the best tools bring the best results and prove most practical in the long run. And so it is with frames for hooking. A good, sturdy frame can be one of your best investments. It not only facilitates hooking but also lets you enjoy the craft to the fullest. It will last a lifetime, besides. Although lap frames are available, a strong frame that stands solidly on the floor is best for making a rug, since a rug steadily increases in weight as it is filled with wool loops.

Don't be a neatnick and hide your frame while a rug is in progress. Friends will be interested in your hobby and will enjoy seeing your rug grow. It may even inspire them to contribute wool. One man and his wife keep "cheek-to-cheek" frames beside a cozy fireplace, a sure sign of togetherness!

The Fraser Frame

This frame, also known as the Bliss Frame, is ideal for hooking. It has many advantages and is the most manageable frame. Mated serrated discs hold it together securely, and the height of the frame is adjustable (see Fig. 3).It can be collapsed into a flat position for storing, when not in use, and for easy transportation in an automobile. The rug bars are moveable, so that once the pattern is attached to the bars, it can be rolled to any area you wish to work on. The forty-inch rug bars are adequate for most rugs and permit the frame to fit into any car. (See Appendix for suppliers.)

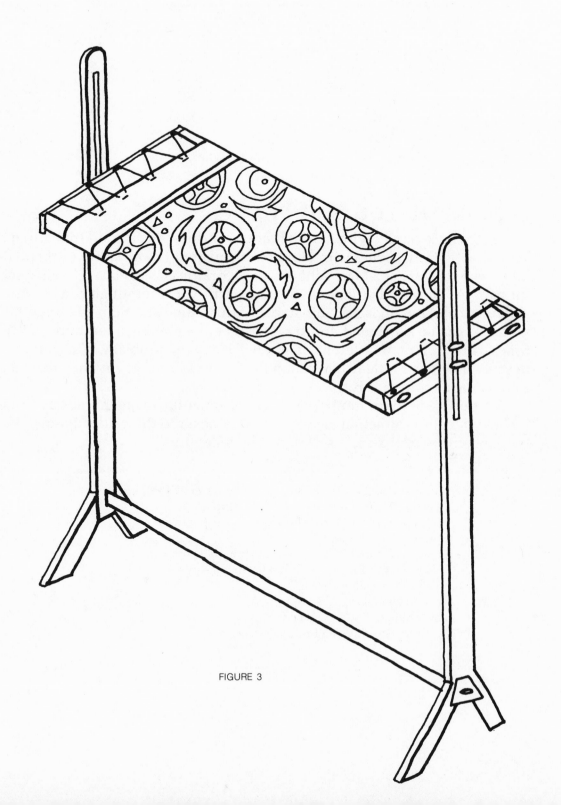

FIGURE 3

A Make-It-Yourself Frame

Anyone who is handy with hammer and saw can make a good frame that can be folded for transportation or storage. If you aren't a carpentry buff and don't know one, inquire at a high-school woodworking class or at a technical school for help. A homemade frame is very satisfactory, even though rug bars are stationary and height is not adjustable. If this frame should be too high for you, legs can be shortened, but try it first, before making alterations. Sometimes using a chair of different height will solve the problem. The frame described here is a little heavier than the Fraser frame, so you may like it better for making a room-size rug.

All wood is standard lumberyard measurements, one inch thick by three inches wide, but the actual measurement is closer to three-fourths-inch by two-and-five-eighths-inches. Ask for the following:

3 pieces 40 inches long, 2 for open-top frame, 1 for tie bar
2 pieces 19½ inches long for sides of top frame
2 pieces 14¼ inches long for inserts on top frame
4 pieces 28 inches long for legs
4 pieces 17½ inches long for cross members for legs
24 No. 8   1¼-inch or 1½-inch flat-head screws
6   1¼-inch nails or brads
Elmer's glue
4 butt hinges 2 by 1½ inches
2   10-inch folding leg braces with screws

The top frame and the two leg frames are assembled by using ordinary lap joints.

To make the open-top frame: Arrange two 40-inch pieces and two 19½-inch pieces to form a rectangle, with longer pieces overlapping the shorter ones at the corners (see Fig. 4). Join them at the corners by gluing them together and inserting wood screws from underneath.

To make the top frame completely flat, so that you can mount your pattern smooth and taut on the frame, glue the 14¼-inch inserts onto the sides of the frame to fill in the space between the two parallel 40-inch pieces. To hold the inserts tight while the glue sets, put in a few brads or nails from the underneath side. Since the drawing is to show basic construction, these inserts were omitted in Figure 4. However, they are necessary to make an even surface for the foundation of your rug.

The two frames for the legs are assembled before joining them to the open-top frame. Join the upper cross members to the legs, using Elmer's glue and wood screws. Notch the two lower cross members in the center of each with a ¾-inch-wide by 1¼-inch-deep notch (see Fig. 5). Join the lower cross members to the legs, with notches on the upper edges of the members, so that the distance from the bottom of the legs to the upper edges of these cross members is 8¾ inches.

With screws supplied with hinges, attach two 2- by 1½-inch butt hinges to upper edges of leg frames, so that pin in hinge is in line with top edge of cross member. The other side of each hinge is attached to the inside edge of the cross arms on the open-top frame.

If you use a cross tie bar (see below), you will need only two folding leg braces for adequate support. Without a tie bar, you will have better support with four braces. Screw the brace to the side of a leg at one end. Then attach

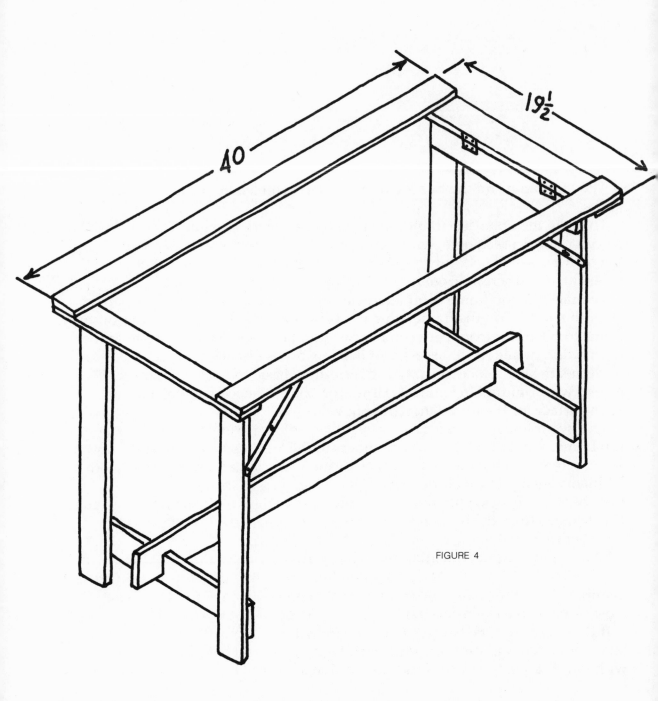

40

$19\frac{1}{2}$

FIGURE 4

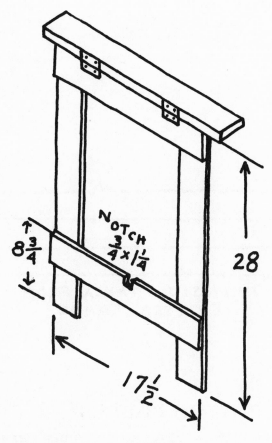

FIGURE 5

the top metal plate of the brace to the underneath side of the top frame. Be sure that when it's opened out straight, the frame and legs are at perfect right angles. Attach the other brace at the other end in the same manner. The hinges and braces permit legs to be folded, so that frame can be collapsed into a flat position, similar to a folded card table.

To make the cross tie bar (Fig. 6): Make a ¾-inch-wide by 1½-inch-deep notch at each end of the tie bar to mate with notches in lower cross members of legs. When frame is erected, cross tie bar can be dropped into notches on cross members and locked into place. Since the bar is removable, screws are unnecessary.

51

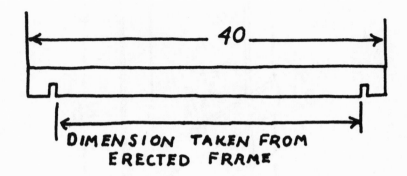

FIGURE 6

Mounting Patterns on Frames

Precision in mounting a pattern will prevent problems later and will insure a straight rug that can't be pulled out of shape while it is held taut during hooking. Follow this procedure for the Fraser frame:

(1) If your pattern is no wider than the rug bars of the frame and does not extend beyond the bars, attach it by sewing it to the bars. This provides the most secure surface for hooking. But first you must wrap the rug bars with 2½- or 3-inch strips of any cotton fabric that can be readily pierced with a needle. Old sheets are not recommended, because it is difficult to push a needle through sheeting. If the fabric tends to ravel, fold under ½-inch on one side of the strip, holding the fold in place as you wrap. Begin at one end of one rug bar by tacking the strip in place, and tightly wrap, round and round, until

52

you reach the other end. Tack that end in place. Repeat the procedure on the other rug bar. Wrappings may remain permanently. With a felt marker, make a bold line on the wrapping in the exact center of each bar. This will be your guide each time you center a pattern. Now you are ready to sew the pattern to the bars.

(2) Locate the center of the pattern by measuring the width from one corner of the *outline* of the rug to the other, on sides or ends that will be attached to the frame. Remember that it is the pattern, not the entire foundation to include margins, that must be centered. A pattern is sometimes stenciled off-center. If it is stenciled so far to one side of the foundation that it cannot be centered on the rug bars, you will have to adjust the center mark accordingly. For example, it may have to be moved three inches to the left or right on each side of the pattern.

(3) The foundation must be perfectly straight on the frame, so check to see that margins are evenly spaced. The outline of the rug and the edge of the foundation, where it will be attached to the bars, should be parallel. If they are not, turn under the edge of the foundation enough to adjust it.

(4) Match the center mark on the pattern with the center mark on one rug bar. Pin or thumbtack it in place. Be sure to mount pattern right side up.

(5) Using carpet thread, or a strong synthetic thread, begin at the center and work toward one end, as you sew the hemmed edge of the foundation to the wrapped rug bar with an overcasting stitch. Remove the pin or tack that was inserted to hold it in place at the center. When the first half is completed, again start from the center of the bar and sew toward the other end. Repeat the procedure to attach the opposite side of the pattern to the other rug bar.

(6) To tighten the pattern on the frame, roll one bar outward, and tighten

the wing nuts that hold it in place. Repeat with the other bar, until the foundation is very taut and the focal point of the rug is centered on the frame. Any slack makes hooking slower.

For a firmer surface, lace the foundation to the side arms that support the rug bars (see Fig. 3). Select ten thumbtacks with one-half-inch shanks; shorter thumbtacks will not hold. Push tacks into each side arm at equal intervals, beginning and ending just clear of the rug bars. (If long tacks are not available locally, see Appendix for supplier. Or you may use upholstery thumbtacks, instead.)

Insert four slender nails, about 2½ inches long, like those used to close up your stuffed Thanksgiving turkey, into each side of the foundation, running parallel to the edge of the foundation, at points halfway between the thumbtacks that are inserted in the side arms.

A practical and durable lacing can be made by cutting 1½-inch-wide strips from an old nylon stocking or panty hose. Pull the strip taut so that it becomes like cord. Knot it securely around the first thumbtack on one side arm of the frame. Pull it tight as you hook it around the first nail in the foundation. Lace back to the second thumbtack, and hook it around the tack without knotting. Continue crisscrossing between frame and foundation, and tie the nylon strip to the end thumbtack. Lace the opposite side in the same manner. This provides a smooth, tight surface for hooking. For safety, poke the ends of the nails to the underneath side of the foundation.

Whenever you wish to roll the pattern to another area for hooking, remove the nails in the foundation and loosen the wing nuts on the rug bars. (The thumbtacks in the side arms remain in place.) After rolling to a new area,

54

tighten the rug bars and again insert the nails in the foundation. Lace with the nylon strips, which remain tied to the end thumbtacks.

As a foundation becomes thick with loops, it is more difficult to roll it taut. To eliminate slack each time you roll the rug bars, tighten the wing nuts to hold them steady, and gently press on the foundation along each bar to ease out slack. Again, loosen the wing nuts and tighten the foundation to take up the slack pressed out.

Although sewing a pattern onto the rug bars of a Fraser frame is the best way to mount it, this can't be done when the pattern is wider than the bars. A wider pattern must be attached with one-half-inch thumbtacks. You can, of course, thumbtack a small pattern to the bars of a Fraser frame for quick mounting and lace it in the usual way to the side arms. Some rugmakers always tack their patterns, but sewing is the better way and the results are well worth the few extra minutes it takes to do it right.

If your rug bars have been wrapped, as described above, do not remove wrapping for thumbtacking. Once they are wrapped, the covering remains. And it is unnecessary to remove the thumbtacks inserted in each side arm for lacing. Loosen the wing nuts that hold frame top in place, and flip the top over to the opposite side, where the side arms are free of thumbtacks. Next time you wish to sew a pattern on, flip top back to the side with tacks.

If you use a homemade frame with stationary rug bars, a pattern must always be tacked, instead of sewn, to the bars, since the bars do not roll. However, if a pattern fits within the bars, it can be first tacked to the rug bars and then laced to the side arms, the same as on a Fraser frame. Very large or room-size patterns must be tacked, regardless of the kind of frame used.

Tack one side of the pattern to a rug bar, beginning at the center and working toward the ends. Insert thumbtacks every two-and-a-half or three inches. Pull the pattern taut as you attach it to the opposite rug bar in the same way. You need plenty of tacks to eliminate any slack areas. Wherever you insert a tack, form a pleat in the foundation, making three thicknesses, to prevent strain on it. And follow a thread of the foundation to keep it in shape.

After the pattern has been tacked to the rug bars, tack it to the side arms in the same way, forming pleats for thickness and following the weave. When you make a very large or room-size rug, the excess foundation that hangs over the bar, on the side where you work, gets in your way, making it difficult to reach underneath the pattern with the hand that holds the wool strip. For easier hooking, fold the part that hangs over and bring the edge up to the rug bar. Insert just enough thumbtacks to hold it. Once more, on the side toward you, fold the portion that hangs over, bringing it up to the bar, and insert a few more tacks.

When you are ready to begin a new area of a pattern that is tacked on a frame, remove all thumbtacks. Shift the foundation to the area that you want to hook next. Again, with thumbtacks, attach the pattern to the four sides of the frame. However, when it is necessary to insert thumbtacks in an area that has been filled with loops, *do not form a pleat*. This would damage your rug. Instead, carefully insert the tacks between loops.

Height of Frame for Hooking

If you have a Fraser frame, adjust the height for comfort in hooking. This will depend on your own height and the height of your chair. When working at a frame that is not adjustable, find a chair that provides the right height. You should be able to rest your arm on the frame without lifting the arm at the shoulder. If your shoulder feels strained, the frame is too high. When a frame is too low, your back will tire from bending over it. With experience, you will settle on a height that is comfortable for you. Don't become a contortionist, trying to reach across your frame to hook an area on the opposite side. Stop long enough to turn the frame around, so that the area is within easy reach. And keep the pattern in a horizontal position, instead of tilted.

If you pay a little attention to position, you will enjoy hours of hooking without discomfort. And a hobby that gives you a backache is no fun.

CHAPTER **6**

The Handy Hook and How to Use It

As soon as your pattern is securely on the frame, smooth and taut, try your hand at hooking. Once you have pulled a strip of wool through the backing and formed a loop, your rug will be in progress. Everyone is awkward at first when learning any new skill, but you will soon feel at ease with a hook.

The Hook to Have and to Hold

The Susan Bates five-inch *straight* rug hook is best for primitive hooking. (Do not order a Susan Bates bent hook. It is difficult to roll the loops off a bent hook.) The hook is flat and large enough to pick up a strip of wool easily. It makes an adequate opening, as it pushes threads apart when inserted in the foundation, to permit the wool to be pulled through without effort. The handle is designed for comfort in the hand. (See Fig. 7.) Ask for the Susan Bates straight hook in needlework and craft shops or department stores, or refer to the Appendix for suppliers.

Cutting Strips of Wool for Hooking

When hooked rugs were first made in this country, the wool strips that form the loops were always cut by hand. Today purists still follow this practice, but cutting machines are available for those who don't like cutting by hand. It is more economical, of course, to cut by hand, without the expense of a cutter. For a big rug, you can cheat a little and combine hand-cut and machine-cut strips, if you wish to invest in a cutter.

To cut by hand: Cut one strip at a time and hook it into the foundation. If you cut a lot of strips in advance, they quickly become tangled and unmanageable. And by alternating cutting and hooking, you will prevent tension as you alternate body positions and movements.

Cut strips lengthwise on the fabric, never on the bias. If possible, tear the fabric before you begin, so that you can follow the straight of the weave when cutting. If the fabric can't be torn, follow a thread as you cut. You may use sewing scraps that run the width of a fabric, such as strips cut from the hem of a dress, if the wool is tightly woven. When using a plaid, you may wish to cut one color that runs crosswise on the fabric. Stripes, too, when cut crosswise, give an interesting effect when hooked.

Don't worry about minor imperfections in your cutting. They become a part of the handcrafted look—and you don't want your rug to look machine-made. But if you find yourself veering too far from the straight and narrow, tear or cut along a thread to establish the straight of the weave again.

Widths may vary according to weight and weave of fabric. Strips are usually cut about ¼-inch wide on medium-weight fabric, such as flannel. The pattern of the rug, too, will indicate how wide the strips should be. There are some fine details even in primitives, and these require more narrow strips. Very thin wool should be cut one-half- to five-eighths-inch wide and folded in half as you hook. Very coarse wool may have to be cut wide to prevent raveling. But if it is unusually thick and heavy, discard it. Any wool that is difficult to pull through the foundation will strain it. Strips twelve to fifteen inches in length are ideal to work with. Longer strips make too many loops without an end, and ends are needed to keep the rug pliable. You can, of course, use shorter strips—anything over three inches long.

To cut mechanically: Mechanical cutters, with blades of different sizes to cut strips of different widths, are for those who do not wish to cut by hand. A No. 6 blade will cut strips three-sixteenths-inch in width. A No. 8 blade will cut ¼-inch strips. Either size may be used for this type of rug. The Bliss cutter is the most convenient to use, because you can set it on a table instead of having to clamp it on. (See Appendix for supplier.)

With Hook in Hand

The technique of hooking is easy enough for a child to master. Once you capture the rhythmic motion, it becomes automatic. Good craftsmanship comes with practice. Don't throw in your hook and abandon your rug just because your first hooking isn't as smooth as you would like. And even if next week's hooking improves noticeably, don't rip out what you hooked this week. After your rug is completed and has been steampressed and walked on a few weeks, it will look as good as anyone else's. Any irregularities become obscured by use.

Practice hooking in straight lines, both horizontal and vertical, and in curves. The design is usually hooked first, because it is the most important feature of a rug. But while you are learning to perfect your skill, hook some background areas first, keeping at least an inch away from any outlines of design. Later, after you have hooked the design, you can fill in these open spaces of background. When you can hook smoothly, alternate between areas of design and background. Don't leave all background until last, because that is the less interesting part to hook.

FIGURE 7

Whenever you rip out an area of hooking, reshape the foundation by gently running the smooth back of the hook over the area, both ways, to pull the fibers back together where they have been pushed apart by the wool loops.

To hook your first loop: Grasp the hook firmly in your right hand, almost as you would hold a table knife while cutting meat. (Reverse hands throughout directions, of course, if you are lefthanded.) The wood handle rests comfortably against the palm or heel of your hand. The extended forefinger, pointed downward, rests against the metal shaft. Your thumb should be against one side of the wood handle (see Fig. 7).

The hook should always be turned up, ready to enter the foundation and scoop up a wool strip.

With your left hand, pick up a strip of wool that has been cut to the desired width. Grasp it between thumb and forefinger, about an inch from the end of the strip. Hold it underneath and against the foundation at the spot where you wish to begin hooking. Use your left index finger to keep the strip flat, where it is held against the foundation underneath. The left hand is always underneath the foundation while you hook (unless you are left-handed and have to reverse the procedure). The last three fingers of the left hand should be loosely curved so that the strip of wool rests lightly on those fingers, with the end dangling from your hand. As you hook, the strip will glide slowly through your curved fingers.

From the upper side of the foundation, push the hook through an opening *between threads,* at the spot where the strip is held underneath and against the foundation (see Fig. 8). If you should split a thread, carefully remove your hook and insert it beside the thread. Wool hooked through split threads will weaken a rug in those spots.

The hook should go through the foundation just far enough to scoop up the wool strip. Don't try to lay the strip of wool across the hook with the left hand. Let the hook do the work and pick up the strip. Pull the end of the wool through the opening to the right side of the foundation, as you ease the grasp on it with your left hand. Release the loose end from the hook on the upper side at a height of about three-fourths-inch. All ends are pulled to the right side. Later, you will clip the end to the height of loops.

Skip two threads of the foundation and, again, insert the hook to scoop up the strip once more, where it is held in your left hand. Hooking from right to left is the easiest way for most right-handed persons, but you may hook in any direction you like—north, south, east, or west! You will have to hook in all directions while a rug is in progress.

Pull the strip through the foundation again, as you ease the grasp on it in your left hand, and form the first loop beside the loose end (see Fig. 9). The

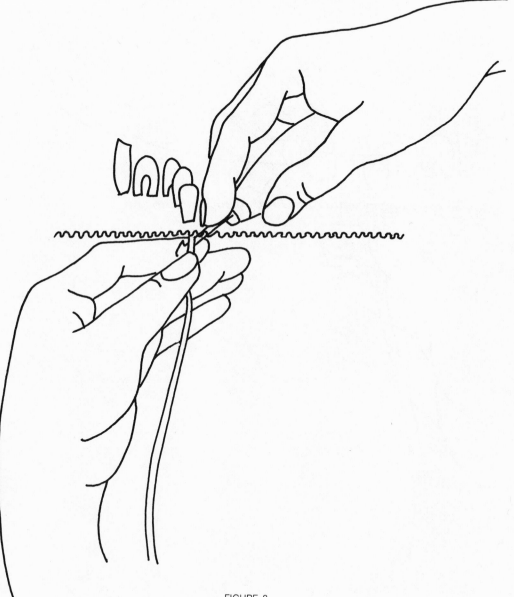

FIGURE 8

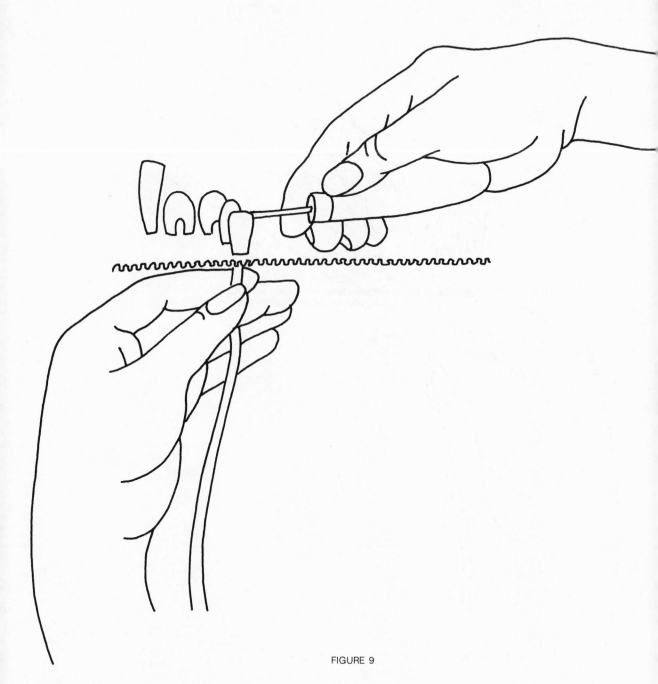

FIGURE 9

usual height for loops is about one-fourth-inch, but some rugmakers pull them slightly higher.

Each time you release a loop, slightly roll the wood handle with your fingers, not your wrist, toward the opposite direction from which you are hooking (toward your last loop). When hooking from right to left, roll to the right. As you roll, the hook turns over and releases the loop. This rolling motion helps to keep loops even and also relieves any strain on your arm and shoulder. Keep strip as relaxed and loose as possible while you work.

At first, you may have to adjust the height of each loop as it is pulled up, but when the technique becomes automatic, you will bring each loop to the height of the others without hesitation. If loops are not high enough, it is usually because of incorrect tension; your grasp on the strip is either too tight or too loose. Don't worry about an occasional loop that is higher—it can be trimmed to uniform height later.

If you catch the foundation with the hook as you bring the wool strip through, you are holding the hook too flat. It should be at an angle approximately forty to forty-five degrees from the surface of the rug.

Continue to insert the hook, skipping two threads each time, as you form one loop against another. (You will choke your rug to death if you try to fill every hole.) When using heavy wool, you may have to skip more than two threads. Some persons always skip three threads. Once you get into the swing of it, you won't count holes but will form the right number of loops by the feel of it. It is better to skip extra threads between loops than between rows. Threads between loops are protected by the wool, while those between rows remain bare and unprotected from dust and wear.

When you reach the end of a wool strip, pull the end through the foundation and leave it on the right side of the rug, just as you did with the end where you began. Do not clip the end until you have begun another strip in that same opening. Then, clip both ends to the height of loops, leaving two loose ends in the same opening.

Hook the next row as close to the first as you can comfortably hook, without straining the foundation, following the contour of the first row. Skip at least two threads of the foundation between rows—more, if necessary, when using heavy wool.

Continue to hook one row against another until an area is completely filled. The loops stay in because of the pressure of one loop against another, as you fill the foundation to form the pile. The final result is a solidly-filled backing and a sturdy, durable rug. No, your rug will not ravel away. Chapters 10 and 11 will tell you more about the directions in which you can hook patterns and backgrounds.

When you have to double thin wool for added thickness, hold the folded edge away from you, toward the hook. The hook will catch the folded edge, instead of the raw edge, for pulling it through. The strip will continue to come through the foundation folded, each time you form a loop.

Avoid packing your foundation too tight. An overload of wool strains and weakens the foundation. You should be able to pull strips through easily. If you can't, it means that loops are too close together. Crowding loops is often a fault of beginners. From time to time, test the suppleness of the rug with your hand. It should be soft and pliable. When you look at the underneath side of a rug, you should be able to see small spots of foundation. If you cannot see the foundation, you have filled it too tight.

For smooth hooking: Never pull a strip of wool across a hooked area underneath to reach an open area. Instead, pull the strip through to form a high loop. Snip it to the height of others, and, with the remainder of that strip, begin a new area. (Whenever you cut a loop, shear it from the top, instead of slipping the blade of the scissors through the loop.) The underneath side of a rug should be perfectly smooth, without twists or crossovers. It will wear better and look neater.

For a tidier hooking nook, drop your clippings into a little basket or box. Or, place an old sheet under your frame to catch them. This makes cleaning up quick and easy.

CHAPTER 7

Why Dye?

The most unappealing fabrics can be transformed into a source of handsome woolens for hooking through the miracle of dyeing. It not only salvages wool that would otherwise be unuseable but also adds to the creativity of rugmaking. You can reproduce colors from wallpapers, fabrics, or paintings to extend the decorating theme of your home in a way that isn't possible through commercially manufactured rugs.

A few beginners shun dyeing, only because they envision a messy process that requires plastic aprons, rubber gloves, goggles, and standing over caldrons of boiling dye. But dyeing is a simple procedure for rugmakers, who dye in comparatively small quantities and usually learn to keep a pot of dye simmering on one burner while dinner simmers on another—keeping a safe distance between the two.

Your dyeing may occasionally produce unexpected results; yet that's half the fun, especially when surprises become assets. The most bizarre colors sometimes bring interesting effects when used in small quantities as accents. But if a color is hopelessly out of step with your color sense, simply overdye the wool, or remove the color and dye it again.

Old Versus New Wool

New wool, professionally dyed, may be purchased for a rug, but a rug made entirely from brand-new wool will never have the charm, the character, and the sentimental value of one made at least partially from cast-off garments of family and friends. Often new wool is not precisely the hue and value that you seek, so it may be desirable to overdye it to get the color you want.

Besides, you mustn't assume that all commercially-dyed fabrics are color-fast. If you doubt the fastness of any color, set the color before using it. Place the wool in boiling water that contains one-third cup vinegar and one heaping tablespoon kosher salt for every one-fourth pound of wool. Simmer the wool for twenty minutes. A rug can be ruined by an overturned glass of water if colors should bleed.

Safety in Records

Keep complete records of dyeing for each rug, along with samples of wool before and after dyeing. Write down proportions of both wool and dye. Don't trust to memory. The more complete your record, the better reference it will provide for future dyeing.

Today there are dyes for wool on the market in many color variations. Dyeing can be done quickly and easily, and colors remain beautiful throughout the life of a rug. What little fading occurs only adds to the beauty of a rug by mellowing and softening its color.

Early-day rugmakers didn't have it so easy. They had to make their own dyes by boiling nature's provisions—beets, berries, flowers, wild grapes, peach leaves, roots, barks, nuts, and onion skins—after having raised the sheep to provide wool for making the fabrics to be died. Yet these ingenious craftsmen created rich colors that endured. Antique rugs displayed in museums are proof of their skill. Some purists are now getting back to making their own dyes; there are books on the subject available in bookstores and libraries.

Cushing Perfection Dyes are preferred by most contemporary rugmakers. A superior product, Cushing dyes come in a wide range of colors and the dyes are made to last. Many craft teachers sell these dyes, but if you cannot purchase them locally, see the Appendix for sources. (The Cushing Company provides a dye color card for twenty-five cents.)

To understand more about colors and how they are related to each other, go to a paint or craft shop and purchase a color wheel.

Here is a good selection of dyes to have on hand:

Blue-Reds
American Beauty
Garnet
Cherry

Yellow-Reds
Egyptian Red
Scarlet
Turkey

Blue-Greens
Reseda Green
Green

Yellow-Greens
Bronze-Green
Bright Green

Blues
Sky Blue
Turquoise Blue

Yellows
Old Gold
Yellow

Brown
Golden Brown
Seal Brown

Orange

Bright Purple

Khaki Drab
Black
Taupe
Silver Gray
Woodrose

Though the Cushing Company makes many color variations, with the above assortment you can achieve almost any color you can think of. You might even begin in a smaller way with fewer dyes. For instance, if you have an aversion to purple, eliminate it from the list. Or if you prefer yellow-reds to blue-reds, eliminate the latter. You can combine dyes to make additional colors. Remember your childhood paint box in school and how you mixed colors? You can do the same with dyes. Red and blue make purple. Yellow and blue make green. Red and yellow make orange. Red, yellow, and blue make brown. But if you use a lot of certain colors, it is really easier and just as economical to have them ready-made for the dye pot.

You can make additions gradually to your dye supply, but you will learn with experience to produce many different effects with a moderate number of dyes.

There is more equipment you will need for dyeing. Lay in some of the following items:

Wetting agent, such as Plurosol, an organic detergent. This causes water to penetrate fabrics thoroughly, so that wool will absorb the dye. It may be purchased from any teacher of rugmaking who sells Cushing dyes (or see Appendix). As a substitute for Plurosol, you may use a laundry detergent, preferably without a bleaching agent.

Kosher salt, because it is pure. Serves as a mordant, or fixative.

White vinegar, also a mordant for setting colors. Cheaper when purchased by the half gallon.

Dye pots. One four-quart and one eight-quart enamelware pot will take care of all your dyeing. Select pots lined with white enamel, so that you can clearly

71

see the color of the wool as you dye. The pots should be cleaned of any dye that clings to the sides after each use to avoid tainting the next dye lot.

Metal tongs, for lifting the wool from the boiling dye to check color and for turning it in the dye pot from time to time.

Small screw-top glass jars, such as jelly jars, to hold liquified dyes. Between dyeings, keep jars sealed well to prevent evaporation.

Felt marker or gum labels, for labeling jars.

Metal measuring spoons, to measure one-fourth, one-half, and one teaspoon, and one tablespoon. There are special spoons that measure one-sixteenth teaspoon and one-thirty-second teaspoon. They are not essential but are occasionally helpful in working out precise dyeing formulas.

Clear glass measuring cup.

Small scale, such as postage, baby, or food scale, for weighing wool. A scale is not essential, but it provides the only accurate measure when dyeing wool of different textures.

Notebook or card file, for permanent records of dyeing. Keep pencil or pen handy.

Tin box, for storing envelopes of dry dye and Plurosol to prevent them from absorbing moisture.

White paper towels. Handy for cleaning up spills and to dip into dye pot to see color before submerging wool.

Removing Color Before You Dye

Fabrics that are too bright or too dark to be overdyed satisfactorily can be salvaged by first removing their color and then dyeing them in a color that you prefer. Even if all color isn't removed, a fabric will usually lighten enough for redyeing. Or it may be used in its lightened form, if you set the color with vinegar and kosher salt.

Experiment with a control sample to find out how a fabric reacts to color removal. If you're not ready to remove color from the entire piece of wool at that time, pin the control sample to the rest of the fabric with a note saying how you removed the color. Divide any large quantities of wool into smaller lots that will fit into your dye pots. Don't crowd wool in the pot when you are removing color.

The easiest way to lighten or remove color from a fabric is to boil it for ten minutes in detergent, using proportions of one teaspoon of any laundry detergent that contains a bleaching agent to every quart of water. Make enough of the solution to cover the wool amply in the pot. Most fabrics will bleach easily in detergent, sometimes becoming almost white. Some commercial processes dye fabrics permanently, however, and it is almost impossible to release the color. If insufficient color is released by detergent, the procedure may be repeated once more. Stay with your dye pot during the process. If you have to leave it for any reason, turn off your range. Suds have a way of boiling over quickly.

If too much color remains in a fabric, use a commercial color remover. (Do not use a laundry bleach, such as Clorox or ammonia.) Be very cautious and very thorough, because these commercial products tend to remain in fabrics and continue to remove color even after wool is dyed again. There is a danger that your rug will fade after it is on the floor. Half the amount suggested by directions on a package of color remover is usually enough.

After you boil color out of wool, whether with detergent or a commercial color remover, rinse the wool very thoroughly in clear warm water to remove both chemicals and the released dye. You may then redye the wool, following directions for dyeing and setting color. (See Chapters 8 and 9.) If you redye wool while it is still wet, there is no need to soak it in a wetting agent. If you wish to use wool as it is lightened, without overdyeing it, set the color that remains in exactly the same way as you would in newly dyeing. If you do not set it, the color will continue to fade after your rug is in use.

Black or brown wool can be treated to look mellow and aged by boiling it in detergent. If insufficient color is released, hang it in the sun for a week or two after loosening the color and without setting it. After further fading by the sun, wash the wool thoroughly and set the color with vinegar and kosher salt in the usual way.

CHAPTER 8

Easy Dyeing for Backgrounds and Other Large Areas

Wool that you have dyed yourself is usually best for backgrounds, because you can control dyeing to provide not only the color and value desired but also shaded effects that break up the sameness of large areas. Commercially-dyed wool does not have this variation. Also, you can combine diversified fabrics by overdyeing them in the same color.

Overdyeing is recommended even when you purchase new wool by the yard (often necessary for large areas) to provide subtle shadings. Sometimes a weak solution of dye in a color near that of the wool will transform it sufficiently for interesting variety. Or you may wish to dull colors that are too bright.

How to Estimate Quantity of Wool to Dye

Before dyeing, you have to know how much wool you will need for the areas you wish to fill. There are two methods of estimating—by weight and by square feet. But since neither way is totally accurate, the safest rule is to dye more than you think you will need. Any surplus will give you a headstart on your next rug.

Weighing wool is the most accurate way of estimating how much you will need. One half pound will hook approximately one square foot. But be aware that this method varies with different textures and also according to how wide you cut strips for hooking as well as how high you pull the loops. When you're thrift-shopping for wool, remember that a wool skirt usually weighs five or six ounces. A yard of new wool weighs about three-fourths pound, differing, of course, with variations in width.

To estimate by square feet, multiply the size of an area to be hooked by four. In other words, for every square foot to be hooked, you will need at least four square feet of wool. But since very thin wool must be cut wider, you would need more of it. And, again, the height of the loops will affect the measurement too.

How to Match Dye Lots Accurately

Dye enough wool for the entire background before you begin to hook. Don't be caught short on the home stretch. You can dye in as many different dye lots as necessary, matching color, by repeating the same measurements of wool and dye. (Measure or weigh wool before it is wet.) Fabrics must be near the same color before dyeing, if they are to match afterward. It is not objectionable, however, if dye lots vary slightly. In fact, the variation becomes an asset when you blend them together as you hook, alternating light and dark values, to give a mottled or shaded appearance. Avoid last-minute dyeing. If you are down to the last corner of a background and need more wool, it will be too late to blend it with the other dye lots. And a difference in dyeing will appear as an obvious, mismatched spot, where the wool is hooked into just one area.

Guard against running short by dividing wool for the background of a rug into four equal parts, mixing different dye lots. Hook one quarter of the wool into one quarter of the background, working from the center toward the outer edge, or from outer edge to center. You can always substitute different wools, if needed, at either of these points but not halfway between. If the wool fails to fill one-quarter of the background, immediately dye more; or purchase more if you are using new, commercially-dyed wool. Don't be tempted to dip into the three-quarters reserved for the rest of the background. Though many antique rugs are tagged as charming or whimsical because of ingenious ways their creators filled in the gaps with anything available, your rug will look better if different textures and dye lots are distributed evenly.

Dyeing by weight is the most accurate method for matching dye lots, especially when you dye different textures and when you dye odds and ends of wool in various shapes and sizes that cannot be accurately measured in inches or feet. Weighing is the only way that you can equalize the quantity of wool in each dye lot, and this is essential for true matching. For example, you can dye a half pound of thin wool in one pot and a half pound of thick wool in another pot, using the same quantity of dye for each. Because they weigh the same, the two different textures will match in color and value, if they are the same color to begin with, even though the two pieces of fabric will not measure the same in square feet. They cannot be dyed in the same pot, however, because thin or loosely-woven wool absorbs dye more quickly than thick or tightly-woven wool.

If you do not have a scale, you can achieve a fair degree of accuracy in matching dye lots by using a paper pattern as a guide for measuring assorted scraps of wool of like textures but unmatched in shape and size.

A strip of medium-weight wool, eighteen-by-thirty-six-inches, weighs approximately one-fourth pound; so cut your guide from heavy brown wrapping paper to this size. Cover the paper pattern with pieces of wool, fitting them together without overlapping, like a jigsaw puzzle. You will then have the equivalent of one piece of fabric in that size. (Cover the paper twice if you wish to dye a larger quantity.) You can match dye lots by continuing to cover the same paper pattern each time and by using the same quantity of dye. Expect some variation if you combine different textures.

When dyeing wool purchased by the yard, simply measure the piece to be dyed with a tape measure, or continue to use your paper pattern. Don't forget to keep records of measurements for the next dye lot.

When working out a desired color for a background or other large area, dye one-fourth pound as a control sample. Always work with pieces of fabric that are longer than their width, so that the lengthwise weave of the fabric is evident. Avoid squares. A practical size to handle is about twelve by fifteen to eighteen inches.

Wait for your control sample to dry before dyeing more wool like it. It will dry one value lighter. If the sample is too light when dry, redye it, adding just enough dye to achieve the desired value. When redyeing, repeat all directions for dyeing, from wetting agent to setting. Correct your permanent record to show the additional dye used. If the control sample is too dark, dye a new sample, using less dye. Unless it is much too dark, the first sample may be hooked against the design in the center of the rug, where a slightly darker background is not noticeable. To dye one value deeper, double the amount of dye when working with light to medium values. To dye one value lighter, use half the quantity of dye.

Dyeing, Step by Step

Always remember that it is the quantity of dye, whether liquified or dry, in the dye pot, together with the quantity of fabric to be dyed, that determines the intensity of the color. The determining factor is not the quantity of water in which the wool is dyed, though many people think this. Water has no effect on the strength of the color, except when you are liquifying dye for easier use. (See Step No. 2 below.) The quantity of dye that penetrates the fabric is the controlling ingredient. The water is merely a medium for causing the dye to enter the fabric.

Begin with clean wool. If you are using an old garment, wash out any cleaning fluid and soilage with a mild detergent. Rinse it thoroughly.

Don't be a cowardly dyer. It is best to dye no less than one-fourth pound and no more than one-half pound at one time. Directions given below are for one-fourth pound. Double all ingredients for one-half pound. Don't be faint-hearted at the idea of plunging this much wool into the dye. Though you may occasionally fail to achieve a desired color, your "failures" are never losses. Whatever you can't use in one rug will build up your supply of dyed fabrics to provide a choice selection when planning color schemes for other rugs. It's also a more efficient use of time to dye in quantity, because it takes just as long to dye one ounce as to dye one half pound. Now proceed as follows:

1. To Prepare Wool for Dyeing

Weigh or measure one-fourth pound wool fabric. Dissolve one-half teaspoon wetting agent, either Plurosol or laundry detergent (see page 71) in very warm water in any kind of utensil. This makes a light suds for soaking the fabric.

However, if it is used fabric that you have just washed or from which you have just removed the color, further soaking is unnecessary, if it is still wet. Open any folds so that water will penetrate wool throughout. The wetter it is, the better it will absorb dye. Wool from old garments requires no more than a five-minute soaking. New fabrics require longer. If they are thick and closely woven or treated with soil repellents, soak them for several hours. An additional one-fourth teaspoon of Plurosol will help.

Do not rinse out Plurosol before submerging wool into dye, but thoroughly rinse out detergent, because most detergents contain a bleaching agent.

2. To Prepare Dye
Ignore directions on packages of dye. A safer technique of dyeing wool for rugs is given here. After selecting your color, measure one-half teaspoon dry dye into a clean measuring cup. Add one cup boiling water and stir well. It is at this time, when liquifying dye, that the quantity of water does affect its strength. By adding only one-half cup water, the dye would, of course, be twice as strong. By consistently using the same proportions, you will always know the strength of any dye that you have liquified, and you will avoid mistakes in measuring. This is a weak solution but an easy one to work with when establishing color of a control sample, especially if you are a beginner and unfamiliar with dyes. If you have to use many teaspoons to reach the color you want, convert your measurements from teaspoons to tablespoons when dyeing more wool. (Three teaspoons equal one tablespoon.)

3. To Prepare the Dye-Pot
Fill the dye-pot two-thirds to three-quarters full of fresh water and bring

80

water to a boil. Add liquid dye from jar by teaspoonfuls, gradually, until you have what appears to be enough dye. Better to dye too light than too dark, because wool can be easily darkened with more dye. As you empty the spoon, dip it into the water so that no dye remains on it.

Immediately record the number of teaspoonfuls of dye used, for future reference.

Add one heaping tablespoon kosher salt to the dye pot and stir well. The salt, along with white vinegar to be added later, makes the dye permanent.

4. Into the Pot

Squeeze out excess water from wool that has been soaking in wetting agent. For a mottled or shaded effect, squeeze out as much water as possible without wringing it. For even dyeing, wool should be very wet when submerged in hot dye.

As you place wool in boiling dye, use metal tongs to move the fabric about, opening folds to permit dye to flow through all areas. Stir occasionally with tongs. For a mottled effect, crowd the wool in the pot and let it boil up slightly above the water line. Though subtle shadings are usually desirable, you will occasionally need to dye evenly, for example, in dyeing wool for geometric patterns. For uniform dyeing, do not crowd wool; keep it submerged at all times, stirring frequently.

Simmer wool in dye for ten minutes and then check color. As the fabric absorbs dye, the water will begin to clear. If the color is not dark enough when all dye is absorbed, add more liquid dye at this time. Stir quickly as you add more dye, so that the entire fabric is darkened instead of just one spot.

When the color pleases you, add one-third cup *white* vinegar to set it.

Vinegar also aids in absorbing any remaining dye in the water. Stir quickly with tongs, moving fabric about, so that dye and vinegar will flow through all areas. After adding vinegar, simmer wool fifteen minutes longer for light values and twenty minutes for dark values.

When wool is slow to absorb dye, an additional one-fourth cup vinegar will help. Usually, all dye will finally become absorbed and the water will clear. But if some dye remains in the water, let fabric cool in the dye before rinsing it for a slightly darker value.

If you are trying to duplicate the color of another piece of wool, place a small cutting from the piece to be matched in a white china cup of water to show color while wet. Whenever the fabric you are dyeing matches the sample you are duplicating, remove it instantly from any remaining dye. Place it in clean, boiling water with salt and vinegar to set it. Simmer fifteen or twenty minutes.

5. To Rinse Dyed Wool

When wool is ready to be rinsed, move the dye-pot from stove to sink. Run warm water into the pot to temper the boiling water, unless you have already let it cool in the pot. Then gradually cool it to lukewarm with cold running water. Rinse the wool and pour off all water. Continue rinsing it in lukewarm water, changing water as many times as necessary, until excess dye and vinegar are washed out.

Squeeze fabric, without twisting, to remove excess water. It is best to line-dry wool, instead of using an automatic dryer; but you may spin-dry it to remove some water and then line-dry it.

Never press wool that is to be used in a rug. The lighter and softer it is, the better to hook with. Don't worry about wrinkles. They disappear in hooking.

Why liquify dye? Though some experienced dyers put dry dye directly into the dye-pot without first liquifying it, this practice is risky, especially for beginners. Dry dye packs a lot of power and is more difficult to control. However, when dyeing for some special effects (see Chapter 9), dry dye may be used.

Whenever you finish using a liquified dye, pour any that remains into a glass jar and identify the color with a felt marker or gum label. The top should be tight to prevent evaporation, which would change the strength of the dye. Mark the water level on the jar. Next time you use it, check the water level. If evaporation has occurred, add boiling water to bring the level back to the water line.

CHAPTER 9

Dyeing for Special Effects

Through variations in the basic dyeing process, you can produce unusual effects and color combinations that make rugs more beautiful.

The Stew

A stew means a combination of fabrics of different textures and colors, dyed together in the same pot. The final result is a variety of colors and values, some bright, some dull. Though different, they are related. A green stew can provide a handsome variety of greens for leaves throughout a floral design. A yellow stew can produce many yellows and golds for flowers. In fact, "stewing" is the best method of dyeing for the pattern of a rug, because it produces such an interesting assortment of wool for individual motifs.

Light colors—yellow, gray, light blue, and beige—dye well together. But light colors cannot be combined with very dark colors, which tend to bleed and change the color of the dye. Tweeds sometimes bleed too, so it's wise to combine them in a separate stew. When dyeing pastel fabrics, use dyes that are grayed, such as olive-green, Egyptian red, American Beauty, or old gold, instead of bright, clear colors. But for a stew that starts with medium gray and tan fabrics, use more brilliant dyes, or the final results will be too dull. A medium-gray wool, overdyed with chartreuse, becomes a pretty yellow-green. If a stew is too bright, add a speck of black or the complement of the color of the dye. The following colors soften each other, as one neutralizes the other: red and green, blue and orange, yellow and violet.

Following are directions for making a stew:

(1) Divide one-half pound assorted fabrics into three groups: light, medium, and dark values. Do not soak them first in Plurosol or other wetting agent, unless they are brand new.

(2) When water in dye-pot is boiling, add one-fourth teaspoon dry dye for one-half pound wool, without first liquifying dye, if you want medium values. Increase the dye to one-half teaspoon dry dye for darker values. When using pastel dyes, you may need even more, since they are very pale. But with dark dyes, such as navy blue, maroon, dark brown, or mahogany, one-fourth teaspoon dye is usually enough.

(3) Add one-half teaspoon Plurosol directly to the dye-pot. (If you do not have Plurosol, soak fabric first in one teaspoon detergent and rinse wool well before putting it into dye.)

(4) Add two heaping tablespoons kosher salt. Stir well. Add darkest wools first to boiling dye, while dye is strong. Simmer for one or two minutes. If fabric absorbs dye quickly, one minute is long enough.

(5) Next, add fabrics of medium values, and simmer for one or two minutes longer.

(6) Add lighest values last, and simmer ten minutes longer.

(7) Add two-thirds cup white vinegar, and simmer the wool for fifteen minutes. For a dark stew, simmer twenty minutes.

(8) Rinse wool thoroughly, according to directions on page 82.

Nature's white flowers are not really pure white. Whatever the species, each has a tinge of color, usually yellow or green. To capture this subtlety for white flowers in a rug, add a piece of white wool at the very end of a stew, when only a touch of dye remains to be absorbed. The wool will take on just enough color to soften the white. The dye that remains from a bronze-green or khaki-drab stew is especially good for this purpose.

Spot-Dyeing

This is a method of dyeing solid-color fabrics in two or three different colors, to produce a variegated or multicolored effect, pretty wherever lines need to be softened. Combine no more than three colors on one piece of fabric; and the colors should be of similar values, rather than ranging from light to dark. For medium to light values, fabrics in light colors—gray, beige, or pastels—are easiest to work with.

If you prefer, spot-dye with only one color, such as black on brown or blue on green. You can dull a bright red wool by spotting it with khaki-drab to produce a variety of values on the one piece. Or spot-dye red with mahogany. Orange dye spotted on gray fabric will produce a variety of brown areas on the gray.

Pieces of wool should be no larger than four by fifteen inches, or they will be too cumbersome to handle. But you may have as many as ten or twelve layered pieces, depending on the size of the pan and how much you wish to dye. Spot-dyeing requires more skill than any other dyeing, so follow the directions below carefully. You can see results instantly, and if colors do not please you, they can be changed before you spot a second piece.

(1) Soak fabric thoroughly in Plurosol. When you are ready to dye it, rinse

out some, but not all, of the suds. If you do not have Plurosol and are using laundry detergent as a wetting agent, rinse out suds thoroughly.

(2) Have envelopes of dry dye open and ready for use. Choose bright-color dyes for spotting, because colors will dull each other. Reserve lightest color till last.

(3) Bring to boil a small quantity of water, about two cups, in a *shallow* pan. Do not use your usual dye-pot, as wool must be crowded in pan. Keep water shallow, but have more hot water ready to add when some of the water boils out.

(4) Add one-half cup white vinegar to the boiling water before placing the wool in it, so that dye can be absorbed and set quickly. (Salt is not used in spot-dyeing.)

(5) Have a second pot of boiling water, containing one-half cup white vinegar, on another burner. This one may be your usual dye-pot.

(6) Squeeze water out of wool that has been soaking in wetting agent and lay it in smooth layers in the boiling water and vinegar. The piece of wool you begin with should be just above the water line.

(7) Dip the tip of a wet, metal, dinner-size fork into one of the dry dyes to pick up a minute quantity of dry dye. Rub it on the wet fabric. Press dye into one spot with a stroking motion, as you push the fabric down into a little water. With the back of the fork, stroke the wool in that spot to spread the dye. When sufficient dye has been pressed into one spot, push the area down farther into the water.

(8) Make each area of color at least two inches in diameter. Avoid small dots of color. Dye several spots on the top layer with the same color, leaving clear areas between spots for another color.

(9) Wait till all dye is absorbed and water clears before beginning a second color. If water doesn't clear in a few minutes, add an extra one-half cup vinegar and wait a few more minutes. You may have to add a little more water at this time.

(10) After you have completed spotting one piece of fabric in one, two, or three colors, remove it from the first pan and submerge it in the second dye-pot for setting. Be sure that the wool is well covered in water.

(11) Spot the next layer of wool, just as you did the first one, and add it to the second pot of water and vinegar. Continue in this manner until each layer is spotted.

(12) Simmer all the spotted wool in the pot of boiling water and vinegar for twenty minutes to set the color. Pour off water and rinse wool, as usual, before drying it.

How to Dye Antique Black

For a rich, soft black that is especially nice for backgrounds, combine a variety of wool fabrics for dyeing—bright plaids, checks, tweeds, and also solid colors, such as navy blue, brown, and dark gray. Avoid very light fabrics that would be conspicuously light even after dyeing.

There are several different ways to dye antique black. One way is to add ample quantities of dry bronze-green, olive-green, or khaki-drab dye directly to the dye-pot. (These dyes are made by W. Cushing & Company.) Or you may overdye wool in a strong solution of its color complement: red wool in green dye, blue wool in orange or golden brown dye, or the reverse of these. Brown wool can be dyed with blue or black dye and black wool can be dyed in brown to soften it. Whenever the black is not quite dark enough, add a small quantity of black dye.

The interesting background of the unicorn rug (Color Plate No. 3) was made of nothing but assorted plaids. For one-half pound of wool, all of this solution was used:

1 teaspoon olive-green dye, dry   } Dissolved in
½ teaspoon dark brown dye, dry } 1 cup boiling water
¼ teaspoon black dye, dry

Favorite Light Background

A popular recipe for backgrounds among hooking buffs is one-half teaspoon khaki-drab dye with a small pinch of golden brown and a small pinch of woodrose, dissolved in one cup boiling water.

When this solution is used in small quantities, the result is a soft, light color, more subtle than plain beige or ivory and ideal for light backgrounds. It varies, of course, depending on what you begin with, whether pale gray, off-white, or white wool. But it always provides a perfect foil for any color used in the pattern. The touch of golden brown and woodrose warms the khaki-drab dye.

This recipe can also be used for dark backgrounds. In quantity, it dyes wool a subtle brownish color. Its medium values provide a muted color that is pretty for outlines, leaves, scrolls, and other motifs.

COLOR TIPS FOR DYEING

Color of Fabric	Dye	Result
Medium or dark gray	Orange	Golden brown
Medium gray or tan	Turkey red	Brick red
Medium gray	Yellow	Yellow-green
Medium and light grays	Sky blue	Soldier blue
Dark gray	Chartreuse	Olive green
White or off-white	Small quantity of black	Williamsburg blue
Deep bright blue	Orange	Antique black
Medium clear blue	Silver gray	Gray-blue
Lavender	Bronze green	Gray-green

When you dye pure white wool, colors turn out clear and vibrant. For muted colors, begin with beige, light gray, or off-white wool.

Plain gray wool looks cold. To warm the color, give the wool a wash of blue, green, red, or golden brown (select one of the colors from the pattern), with only a small quantity of dye. The color will remain gray, but it will be more pleasing to the eye.

Any color that is too bright may be muted by using a little khaki, khaki-drab, mahogany, or its color complement. A minute quantity of brown or black dye will also dull a color.

CHAPTER **10**

How to Hook Patterns

The focal point of a rug is the area to hook first. It may be a cluster of flowers, an animal, or a scroll—whatever is the most important feature.

Outlining Motifs

Most motifs within a pattern require outlines in contrasting colors and textures, to define the pattern and for accents that make each rug unique. Hook the outline of an individual motif first, before filling the area within it. Then, hook one continuous row inside and against the outline with the same wool that is to fill the motif. Almost any wool fabric is suitable for outlining—plaids, tweeds, solid colors, smooth and rough textures. Spot-dyed and paisley fabrics are especially pretty to soften lines. Checks may be used if overdyed, but the color combination in most checks is too sharp "as is." Colors and values of outlines are determined by the background, because they must distinctly contrast with it to serve their purpose.

Wherever a contrasting outline is not required (some details are too small for outlining), hook one continuous row all the way around the motif, the same as you would an outline, but in this case you would use the wool with which the motif is to be filled, instead of a contrasting wool. By hooking this row first, you establish a smooth and distinct edge.

Always hook just inside the lines of a pattern, instead of on the lines, unless you are hooking single lines for details, such as stems, vines, or tendrils. If you hook on the lines, you will enlarge your pattern by one row.

Directions given in this chapter are for hooking individual motifs that are frequently found in primitive patterns.

91

Flower Planning

Keep flowers uncomplicated, free of realistic shading and fine details. Mottled dyeing provides adequate shading for primitive flowers. And since realism does not prevail, two different colors or two different species may bloom from the same stem.

STEARNS PRIMITIVE, 20 by 60½ inches, Craftsman pattern No. H288, hooked by Betty Short. The clean composition is typical of primitive designs. This one resembles early crewel. The background was made from a favorite coat of Mrs. Short's—her way of preserving it.

Outlining enhances most flowers, but it should not dominate them. Here are some suggestions for outlines: First, a contrasting color and/or texture, such as brown tweed to outline a blue flower of smooth wool, against a light background. Second, a darker or lighter value of a flower's color, either the same or different texture. A dark red to outline a medium-red flower, against a light background. Or a lighter red to outline a medium-red flower, against a dark background. Or, third, the same color and value as the flower in a distinctly different texture. Heavy gold tweed could outline a gold flower of smooth wool.

Primitive Roses

Traditional floral patterns often feature roses that have more detail than most other primitive flowers. Drawings containing numbers corresponding to the following numbered directions are provided for three different rose designs that are typical of those found in many patterns (see Figs. 10, 11, and 12). (The same key to the numbers applies to all flowers illustrated in this chapter.) Let your imagination soar above stereotyped pink and red roses, and create your own varieties in gold, rust, ivory, mauve, or blue.

(1) Establish the growing line, the division between petals that open out and those that cup toward the center. It may be a darker value of the petals or a contrasting color, such as mahogany or brown on a red rose. (This line is black in many antique rugs.)

(2) Establish the edge by outlining the flower in a different texture, value,

93

FIGURE 10

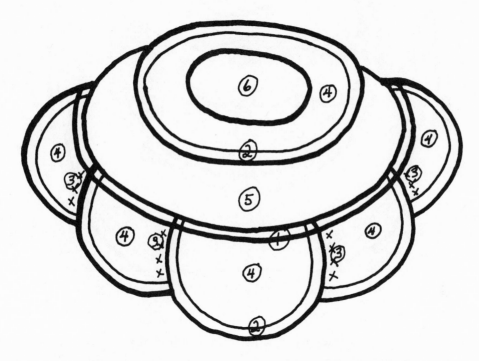

FIGURE 11

or color, depending on background. The contrast must be distinct, so that the flower will stand out instead of becoming lost in the background.

(3) If the outline does not appear distinct and does not clearly define petals, hook one row in a darker value of the color of the flower. These shadow lines are indicated by small crosses in the illustrations.

95

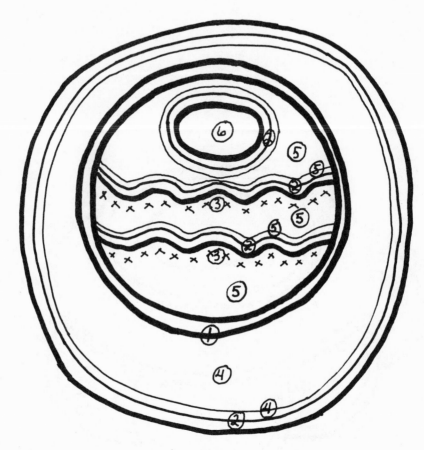

FIGURE 12

(4) Hook one continuous row against the outline of the petals and fill the remainder of this area with the same fabric, establishing the color of your rose.

(5) With a lighter value of the color used in (4), hook one continuous row against the outline and fill the remainder of the area indicated by No. (5). Or you may hook No. (5) in a contrasting color. Many early rugs were treated in this way.

(6) To accent the center of the flower, hook one continuous row in a darker value or contrasting color. Fill the center with a color repeated from another portion of the rug. (See page 100.)

96

Color Plate No. 1. HEN WITH BASKET, 30 by 40 inches, Edana Design No. 148, hooked by Joanna Orton, who dyed the antique black background herself. The chicken, hooked in tweeds, proudly carries a basket of Easter eggs. Mrs. Orton chose to fly the flag of New England. A similar flag was carried during the Battle of Bunker Hill. The hit-or-miss border repeats colors from the pattern.

Color Plate No. 2. PUTNAM HISTORIC, 29 by 44 inches, Craftsman pattern No. 285, hooked by Chipps Smith. The original rug, from which this pattern was adapted, was hooked by Louisa Putnam, a relative of General Israel Putnam of Revolutionary War fame. The Wedding Rug, Color Plate No. 14, was also designed by her. The mammoth cat by the little house implies that the artist had a whimsical bent. Coarse brown and tan tweeds give the cat a shaggy look. The background looks very primitive with its many textures and values. Wool strips were cut unusually wide in this rug.

Color Plate No. 3. UNICORN, 38 by 46 inches, from an original crayon drawing (pattern unavailable) by Tiffany Winslow at age nine and hooked by her grandmother, Edna Hall. A unique unicorn, indeed, with his flowing tail of shocking pink! Only the background was specially dyed for this rug. (See page 89 for details of the dyeing.)

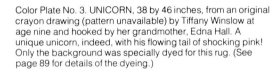

Color Plate No. 4. CLASSIC SCROLLS, 36 by 70 inches, Edana Design No. 168, hooked by Anna Vogeley. A handsome example of scrolls. They are outlined in tweed and have red veins accented by one row of brown. Outer portions of scrolls are beige; inner portions are bronze-green. Flowers are both cardinal red and Egyptian red.

Color Plate No. 5. STAR, Heirloom pattern No. 56 (23 by 38½ inches) and No. 56A (40 by 72 inches), hooked by Mary Sargent. The rug pictured was adapted to 32 by 49 inches. This simple geometric is an excellent choice for a beginner. Stars, outlined in black, are two values of red, dulled with khaki drab. The hit-or-miss stripes run only one way, but the stenciled pattern divides the blocks into four sections. The smaller blocks can be hooked alternately in two directions, vertically and horizontally, giving the effect of a quilt pattern.

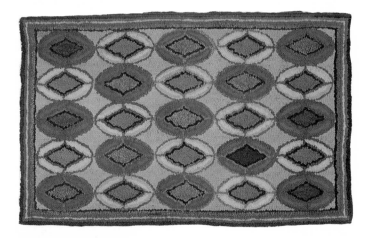

Color Plate No. 6. GEOMETRIC OVALS, 27 by 42 inches, Craftsman pattern No. H228, hooked by Dorothy Hill. Though this is a traditional pattern, bright colors give it a contemporary look. The rug features many textures and values of bright pinks and greens. Different values in the ovals are balanced diagonally. All colors are repeated in the border.

Color Plate No. 7. MARIGOLD HEROIC, 28 by 62½ inches, Heirloom Rugs pattern No. 716D, hooked by Alice Beatty. Though the composition is typical of primitive patterns, the color scheme is contemporary. Copenhagen blue flowers, outlined in a lighter value, are set against a pale yellow-green background. The scroll was outlined in purple plaid.

Color Plate No. 8. GODEY SPRAY (RED BACKGROUND), 18 by 30 inches, Heirloom Rugs pattern No. 573, hooked by Shirley Cull. See Chapter 13 for details on making this rug.

Color Plate No. 9. GODEY SPRAY (BEIGE BACKGROUND), 18 by 30 inches, Heirloom Rugs pattern No. 573, hooked by Fay Kemp. See Chapter 13 for details on making this rug.

Color Plate No. 10. MARINER'S STAR, 28 by 41 inches, pattern No. 43, designed by Lib Callaway, hooked by Mary Sargent. See Chapter 13 for details on making this rug.

Color Plate No. 11. FLAT ROSE DIAMOND, 24½ by 34½ inches, Heirloom Rugs pattern No. 725B, hooked by Alice Beatty. See Chapter 13 for details on making this rug.

Color Plate No. 12. SAILCLOTH PRIMITIVE, 29 by 68½ inches, Heirloom Rugs pattern No. 716L, hooked by Shirley Daley. This handsome pattern with sturdy primitive flowers is a copy of a very old rug hooked on sailcloth. It is said to have been made by a sailor. Background of this rug was dyed with "Favorite Light Background" (page 89) and the flowers with Egyptian red and old gold. The khaki stem in the border has a nice flow. Other stems are very prominent and typical of primitive patterns.

Color Plate No. 13. NEVER, NEVER RUG, 31 by 66 inches, Craftsman pattern No. H98, hooked by Beatrice Ealer. The original rug was one of the oldest in the Burnham collection and, according to tradition, was made of Revolutionary War uniforms. The cat in this rug was hooked to resemble Mrs. Ealer's own pet. The pattern is described poetically:
This is the TREE that never grew,/ . . . the BIRD that never flew,/ . . . the CAT that never meowed,/ . . . the HORSE that never plowed,/ . . . the FISH that never swam,/ . . . the HORSE that never ran,/ . . . the DUCK that never quacked,/ . . . the SQUIRREL that never a nut cracked,/ . . . the FLY that never made butter,/ . . . the BEE that made nary a flutter,/ . . . the GULL that never saw the sea, and/ . . . the LEAF that never made tea.

Color Plate No. 14. WEDDING RUG, 30 by 44 inches, Craftsman pattern No. H275, hooked by Alice Beatty. This sentimental design of hearts and flowers, hooked in old fabrics, could easily pass for an antique rug. The mottled background was made from several different World War I army uniforms. Flowers and leaves of Egyptian red and turquoise are accented by a bold, black stem. Hearts in the corners have been treated in different ways to add to the handcrafted effect.

Color Plate No. 15. NEW HAMPSHIRE ANTIQUE, 42 by 81 inches, Heirloom Rugs pattern No. 530, hooked by Joanna Orton. The original rug is at The New Hampshire Historical Society, Concord, New Hampshire. The composition offers the finest in floral design. Too intricate for a beginner's first rug, it requires a more experienced hand. Some flowers are cardinal red, some Egyptian red. Scrolls are of wool dyed in seal brown.

Color Plate No. 16. NEW BEDFORD, 38 by 60 inches, hooked by Alice Beatty. This pattern was drawn by Ruth Atkinson, South Dartmouth, Massachusetts, from a painting in the Whaling Museum in New Bedford, Mass. A similar pattern, No. 72, is available from Edana. Wool for sky was a mottled gray and white wool that looked like grandpa's longjohns before it was overdyed with a mere tint of dark brown. A tiny bit of crimson was added to the dye for wool used at the horizon. The foreground is gray tweed and plain gray, overdyed with khaki. Windows were filled with light brown wool, spot-dyed with plum. Most of the hooking is in straight rows.

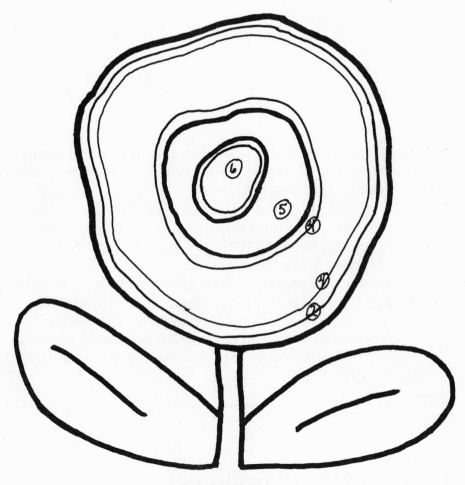

FIGURE 13

Round, Flat Primitive Flower

A simple, flat-looking flower, one of the most popular found in primitive patterns, is often combined with other motifs, such as animals, houses, or hearts. Study Figure No. 13, using the keyed directions for (2), (4), (5), and (6).

No. (2) is the contrasting outline of the flower.

97

No. (4) indicates one continuous row against the outline and another against the inner portion of the flower. These two rows and the area filled between them are hooked in the same fabric.

No. (5) is filled with a lighter value of the color used in No. (4) or with a contrasting color. On very big, round flowers (some are eight to ten inches in diameter), the dividing line between these two portions should be accented with a contrasting fabric to break the flat look.

See pages 100–105 for treatment of center, No. (6), and for leaves and veins.

A very small, round flower does not require an outline, unless it is in a cluster of flowers and would not otherwise be defined. Hook small flowers within a cluster in different values and textures to distinguish one from another. Values may be graduated toward the end of a spray, with the lightest value at the very end.

The Daisy and Similar Flowers

A daisy with an even number of petals may be hooked by filling the petals alternately with two different values of a color, or two different textures, as indicated by (4) and (5) in Figure 14. When there is an uneven number of petals, outline them with a contrasting fabric to define and separate them. Then, fill each petal the same. The center, No. (6), is treated the same as in other flowers. Your daisy may be whatever color you like. And regardless of nature, the center need not be yellow. Make it red, if red looks best.

FIGURE 14

Tubular Flower

The top portion of a tubular flower is the area to emphasize (see Fig. 15). For outlining No. (2), use any contrasting fabric that clearly defines it.

No. (5) is hooked in whatever color you like, but it should be either darker or lighter than the throat of the flower. Hook one continuous row against the outline in the usual way, and fill the area.

To accent the center and to coordinate the flower, hook one row, (4), with the same fabric used for the throat of the flower. The center, No. (6), may be any contrasting color that is darker than No. (5).

If there are stamens, hook them in a color that will highlight them against the flower, such as red against gold or brown against blue.

Notice that the throat of the flower is not outlined with a contrasting fabric in the usual way. The edge is established by hooking one continuous row, using the same wool that fills the throat. The reason is that a tubular flower is cylindrical, so there is no edge to accent in the same sense that you would accent or outline the edge of a petal or even the upper edge of the tubular flower. The color of the throat should contrast very distinctly against the background, either much lighter or much darker.

Centers of Flowers

Leave centers until last, and then select a color from another area of the rug. A very small center should be filled temporarily, when you begin the flower, with any scrap of wool to keep the area open and from becoming obscured by

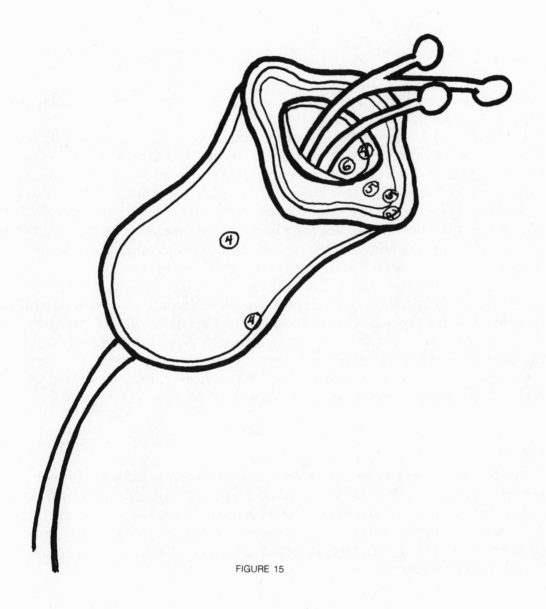

FIGURE 15

the wool loops around it. Pull out the temporary center when you are ready to replace it with a permanent one.

Don't underestimate the power of these little centers. Though small, they affect the overall appearance of a rug. The right one will enhance a flower and the wrong one will detract from it. You may have to try several different colors or textures to find the one that looks best; keep trying until you are satisfied.

Almost any color and fabric may be used, but the color should be subtle to complement the flower. A color may be repeated from another flower. Yellow centers are not predestined! If the center is more prominent than the flower, it is too bright. There is no fast rule, but on a light background, with flowers of medium to dark values, centers would usually be lighter than the flowers. On a dark background, flowers are lighter, so centers would be darker or a little brighter than the flowers. Unless they contrast in color with the background, they will look like background peeking through. When centers look too dull, outline them with a brighter color if they are large enough to take an outline. The same kinds of wool that are suitable for outlining are also suitable for centers—plaids, paisleys, tweeds, or spot-dyed fabrics.

Buds

When hooking a bud, repeat the same color and outline from the flower to which it is related. A bud in the shape of a tight little sheath, with overlapping petals, may be hooked in two values, with the lighter value on the overlapping petal, the darker value on the underneath petal. Hook the little knob, sometimes at the base of a bud, in a medium value of a contrasting color, possibly green or brown.

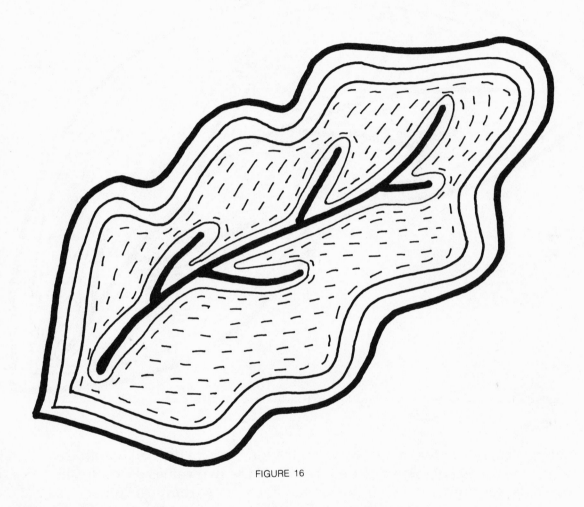

FIGURE 16

Leaves

Foliage may be either a foil for flowers or the main feature of a pattern. Leaves in nature are of many colors—green, brown, gray, khaki, red, or gold. So choose the color you like best in your rug, even one *not* in nature. A large curved leaf, divided by a vein, may be hooked in two different values of one

103

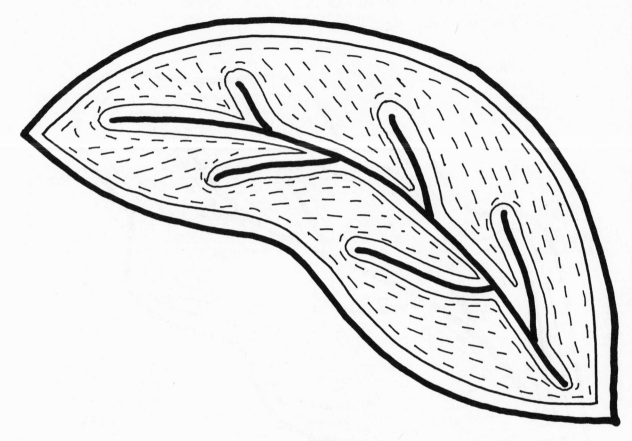

FIGURE 17

color, with the lighter value always on the long side of the curve. If this is done, the outline of the leaf should be one of the two values used, the lighter one if background is dark and the darker one if background is light.

When a leaf is partially hidden by another leaf, the one underneath should be darker in value than the one on top. Or the two may be hooked in slightly different colors, such as yellow-green against reseda-green.

A leaf may be outlined with one, two or three rows of hooking, depending on its size, but very small leaves do not require outlines, unless they overlap and need to be defined. Muted colors, such as brown, khaki, taupe, or beige,

104

make suitable outlines—a soft brown to outline a green leaf or khaki to outline a red leaf.

If there is a vein, hook it before filling the leaf. Then, hook one continuous row around the vein with the wool that is to fill the leaf. Next, hook outward from the vein to meet the outer rows of hooking (see Figs. 16 and 17), or simply fill the leaf without apparent direction.

Just as bones give support to a body, veins give strength to leaves. Unless a leaf is very small, show a distinct vein—one row, hooked on the lines of the vein. The color may be bold but not bright, either darker or lighter than the leaf. Muted hues may be used, as long as they are strong enough in value to be clearly distinguished—soft blues, reds, greens, browns, or grays—depending on the color of the leaf. Or give a blue-green leaf a yellow-green vein, and a yellow-green leaf a blue-green vein.

Almost any fabric is suitable, especially contrasting textures. And all veins throughout the same pattern need not be hooked in the same fabric.

Stems of Leaves and Flowers

Stems, like veins, are a part of the "bone" structure of plants. But they should be hooked in fabrics that differ from the veins. Otherwise, the stems would appear to run through the centers of the leaves. A red leaf with a blue-gray vein might have a charcoal-color stem. The prominence of stems depends on your personal taste and on the design of the rug. They may be played up or down but should stand out clearly from the background. You want a healthy-looking plant with good, strong support. Tweeds are especially suitable, because they give a sturdy look. Many rugs feature stems so bold that they are of major interest. Entwined among leaves and flowers, they give continuity and motion to patterns.

Stems on a light background may be of medium to very dark values. Those on a very dark or black background may be of medium to light values. Stems of large leaves and flowers require two rows of hooking. The row on the longer side of a curve may be one value lighter than that on the inside of the curve. For added interest, the long side may be of a plaid or mottled fabric and the other row plain. And meshing or dovetailing the loops of the second row against the first gives a fascinating effect.

Trunks and Branches of Trees

Though tree trunks and branches are usually thought of as brown, they are actually nearer to dark gray. Select whichever color looks better with the background and other colors of your rug, but it should be strong and bold to stand out prominently against the background.

Trunks and branches in very coarse tweeds give the appearance of rough bark. You may alternate two different tweeds, hooking them in a striated pattern. Or divide the trunk in half, vertically, in an irregular line, and hook one side of the trunk lighter than the other side, as though the sun were hitting it. Branches may be hooked in one value or in two different values, following the usual rule—lighter value on the long side of the curve.

106

Scrolls

Scrolls are featured in many patterns and lend grace and motion to a design. When they are the focal point of a rug, let them dominate the rest of the pattern in hue and values. But when scrolls are merely a frame for a center design, such as flowers or birds, keep them simple.

Hook scrolls in the direction of their flow. Or use the technique of filling, without motion or direction. Since scrolls and leaves are related in form, rules for leaves apply. Scrolls are usually outlined with at least one or two rows of hooking—sometimes more if they are very large. Large scrolls without veins may be outlined with several rows of one color and filled in the center with another color. A soft brown may be combined with soft blue. But don't combine two bright colors. One section should flow into the next without sharp contrasts. Tweeds make handsome scrolls. Plaids are pleasing for veins and outlines.

(See Color Plate No. 4 for a fine example in which scrolls are the main feature of the rug.)

Animals and Birds

Thick, rough textures are more suitable than thin, smooth fabrics for hooking animals and birds, to give a furry or feathered look. Hook in the direction that fur or feathers grow. Outlines in contrasting values or colors will define haunches, paws, ears, or wings—lighter outlines for dark animals and birds, darker outlines for light animals and birds. For example, gray or brown on black animals, dark brown on lighter brown animals.

107

BREWSTER HORN, 28 by 47 inches, Edana pattern No. 19A, hooked by Mary Sargent. The design features three popular motifs—hearts, flowers, and scrolls. The reds, blues, golds, and khakis are distributed throughout the entire rug and well balanced. Most of the fabrics were leftovers from other rugs.

The body of an animal may be softly striated with a darker or lighter value in a different fabric. Tails and manes of horses can be accented by different textures, hues, or values—a black tail and mane on a brown horse, a gray tail and

AMERICAN EAGLE WITH SCROLL, 38 by 63 inches, Karl Kraft Studios, pattern No. 213, hooked by Elizabeth Regenthal. This stately eagle manifests strength and courage. Feathers were hooked in several different gray-and-white tweeds, outlined in dark gray. Head and tail are plain light gray. Claws are pale gold to show how the eagle clutches the olive branch and the arrows. The scroll that frames the eagle is outlined in red-and-black plaid. One half of the scroll was filled with this same plaid and the other half in old gold.

mane on a black horse. Wings and tails of birds may be of either the same or a different fabric, but they must be distinguished from the body of the bird with an outline. Make legs on the opposite side of an animal darker than those in the foreground for better perspective. If you have a pet of your own and want to immortalize him in a rug, reproduce his color and markings. A colored snapshot is a helpful guide.

Eyes are usually big and prominent and may be hooked in white, pale gray or gold with black or dark brown pupils. But pupils are not shown on small animals and birds; just fill the eye with a contrasting color. You may have to try different colors to find the best one. Gold or green eyes are pretty for dark cats and red eyes for some birds. Since the area is small, make the loops for eyes slightly higher than the rest of the animal or bird, so that they will stand out clearly.

If beaks and feet of birds and other small details are of adequate contrast with the background, they won't be lost to the eye. You may hook a dark red, brown, or oxford-gray beak against a light background or a white beak against a dark background.

Strawberries

Big, juicy strawberries are sometimes featured in primitive rugs. When you hook the berries, avoid packing them with too many loops, because you will need space to add the seeds.

Let plenty of dark seeds peep through so that the strawberries can be instantly recognized. Dark red strawberries are pretty with dark gray or charcoal seeds, light red strawberries with medium gray seeds. To hook the seeds, bring one end of a wool strip through an opening, then pull a loop through another opening, as close to the first as possible. Shear the loop and the end slightly higher than the loops of the berry. This leaves two ends without a loop to form a fleck of color that indicates a seed.

The little green fringed caps of the berries are too small to outline, but the points can be defined by alternating two values.

Houses and Other Buildings

After first outlining a house or other structure, hook it in straight, horizontal rows. When two sides are shown, hook one side darker than the other for correct perspective. Make the roof dark. Gray, red, charcoal, or brown is usually best. A door may be of any color you like. The Pennsylvania-Dutch used to paint doors blue as a signal to young blades that they had marriageable daughters within. Why not dream up your own reason for the color of your door?

If you look at a house from the outside, you will see that window areas appear dark. So fill the windows with dark, warm colors—taupe, brown, or plum— to provide a feeling of warmth inside.

You can deviate from nature and make the ground around your house khaki, instead of green. The sky above may be beige instead of blue. Choose the colors that will make the best background for your picture.

111

VENEZIA, 20 by 40 inches, Heritage Hill pattern No. 46, hooked by Nathalie Richardson. A good pattern for a beginner, because it requires only small quantities of each fabric. Pale blue-gray makes a perfect background for the colorful houses. Two values of brown were used for the rooftops to distinguish each one from the next.

Geometric Patterns

Geometric designs have been popular with rugmakers since the early days of this craft. They are pleasing to almost everyone and make suitable companion rugs to those of contrasting design. A geometric pattern is a wise choice for a room-size rug, because it will usually combine well with pattern in draperies or wallpaper.

Old patchwork quilts are an ideal source of ideas for geometrics, and some of the old quilt patterns have been adapted to rugs. Star-shaped patterns are especially popular. (See Color Plate No. 5.) A mosaic pattern, similar to a "crazy" quilt, makes an interesting rug and solves the problem of what to do with scraps of wool in limited quantities. For more interesting hooking, geometric motifs can be alternated with other motifs—flowers, leaves, animals, hex signs and other Pennsylvania-Dutch designs.

Though geometrics are recommended for the novice, colors must be carefully planned for good balance. Three colors are adequate. More may cause a busy look. But you should include five or six values of the colors used, along with plenty of neutrals for variety. Follow the usual rules of gradual changes between values and a diagonal balance. (See Color Plate No. 6.)

Backgrounds of the different blocks or medallions may be the same or different. But, again, remember diagonal balance and gradual change in values. If one block has a dark background, the next should be of medium value, instead of very light. Each block should be boldly outlined to define it. And for a truly finished look, a geometric rug needs a plain, narrow border that repeats one of the colors in the pattern.

A clever trick is to overdye each color to be used in a geometric in a very weak solution of one of the colors selected for the pattern, to give all of them a common denominator that will coordinate them. However, do not dye them together, because the colors might bleed into each other. Colors should remain almost as they were before, except for a very faint tinge or wash of the denominator color. Select a dye that is suitable for the color scheme.

Before beginning a geometric pattern, divide all the wool collected for it into thirds. Complete one-third of the rug at a time, so that colors and textures will be distributed evenly.

Contemporary Patterns

When hooking contemporary patterns, you can put aside rules for graduating values and mutation of colors. These patterns are usually a play of splashy color and feature bold, strong lines. Many early patterns can be treated in contemporary fashion, especially a series of patterns called "Heroics." They are big and bold and can be easily adapted to modern colors. (See Color Plate No. 7, Marigold Heroic.) You may want to go strictly modern with free form and abstract shapes. Some designs simply feature plain, random-size blocks, flagstones, bricks, or swirls of color.

There is little detail, so areas are hooked in solid colors, often intense and striking, though earth tones are also popular among modern enthusiasts. One handsome room-size rug features a dramatic sunburst of color, encompassing the entire rug. As in other forms of contemporary decor, texture is important. Some of the heavier tweeds and herringbones are ideal.

Dates and Initials

When you hook dates or names or initials, use single, wide strips, and hook one number or letter at a time. Immediately, hook one continuous row of background wool around it to hold the shape, before going on to the next.

CHAPTER 11

How to Hook Backgrounds and Borders

After you have hooked some of the design in your rug, begin to hook the background area around it. For a smooth appearance, where background and design meet, always hook one continuous row of background wool around each detail of the design. Also, hook one continuous row of background wool along the four sides of the border or along the outer edge of a rug that has no border.

The direction in which the background of a rug is hooked forms subtle patterns that break up the area. The method you choose depends on personal taste and on the pattern of the rug.

Styles of Hooking

For a background of graceful, flowing curves that lend motion (see Fig. 18), begin by hooking the loops to form a letter S, three to four inches high. Following the contour of the S, hook several more rows against it. Then, begin a new S near the one just formed. Continue to hook in this manner, filling areas between with smaller curves, throughout the entire background. Avoid straight lines, squares, or circles. A background hooked in curves and swirls is suitable for any pattern except a geometric, which requires a static or quiet background.

A background devised by early-day craftsmen and still popular is formed by hooking very straight rows across either the width or length of a rug. The technique is called straight directional hooking. Draw a few broken parallel

FIGURE 18

guidelines on the foundation with a felt marker, several inches apart, to keep rows straight as you hook. On a burlap foundation, you can make guidelines with the dull point of a soft lead pencil; the pencil will easily follow the track between two threads of the burlap. It's wise to hook guidelines first and fill in between them afterward. Each row of straight hooking should be continuous, from one side to the other, except where a row meets an area of design. But don't forget about first hooking a row of background wool around each detail of the design before bringing the straight rows to meet it. Straight directional hooking is suitable for simple, uncluttered patterns with open spaces between areas of design or for rugs with plain centers.

Directional hooking can also be done in waves (see Fig. No. 19). A back-

FIGURE 19

117

ground of wavy lines that run from one side of a rug to the other is a variation of straight directional hooking and is used for the same kinds of patterns. Follow suggestions in the paragraph above, except for making rows waved instead of straight.

Contour hooking is illustrated in Figure No. 20. For a gently striated background, follow the contours of a pattern with row after row of hooking. For example, in a floral pattern, multiple rows of hooking would follow the contours of each flower, leaf and stem. When hooking the background between areas of design, work from both directions to equalize the striations. Taper contours as you near the border. Contour hooking provides motion and is suitable for almost any type of pattern except a geometric. Use the "fill" technique described below to hook very small areas, where there is not enough space to follow contours.

As a variation, you may combine contour hooking with straight directional hooking by first hooking five or six rows to follow the contours of the design. Then, hook the remainder of the background in straight rows.

The Technique of "Filling"

The term "fill" means to cover an area with loops of wool so that there is no direction or motion in that area. No more than three or four loops are pulled through the foundation in any one direction. This method of hooking is used for areas that should appear static, such as windows of a cottage or stars in a geometric pattern. It is also used for small areas between motifs.

FIGURE 20

All About Borders

A border is to a rug what a frame is to a picture. It gives a more finished look and sets off the design, even though it may consist of but a few rows of hooking in a contrasting color or value. Most rugs look prettier with a border, but when a design is contained within a wreath of leaves or scrolls, a border is superfluous. And a very small rug may look better without a border if it would crowd the design. However, rugs with geometric patterns, either large or small, look more finished with two or three rows around the outer edge. Since the edge of a rug is most vulnerable to wear, always use closely-woven fabrics for borders—sturdy but not too thick. Wool that is too thick can cause a rug to cup or look lumpy at the edge.

Plan the border of your rug after the design and most of the background are completed, just as an artist selects his frame after a picture is painted. Begin hooking the border at the outside edge, next to the binding, leaving one thread of foundation between the binding and the first row of hooking. This will make it easier to turn the binding to the underneath side later. Work inward, so that edges will be smooth and even. If there is no border, hook one or two continuous rows of background wool along the four edges before hooking the rest of the background to meet it.

Repeat colors from the pattern in the border, instead of injecting new colors there. Or make the border a deeper or lighter value of the background color. There are many different kinds of borders, featuring chevrons, circles, diamonds, scallops, stripes, squares, or hearts; but following are the most popular designs:

A plain, narrow border, one-half to one-and-one-half inches, may be

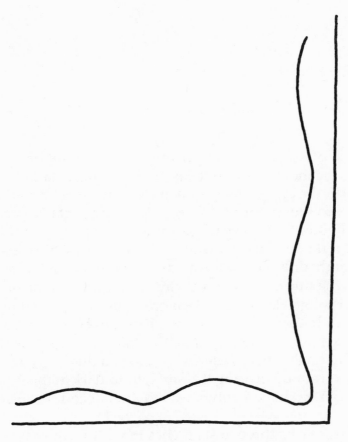

FIGURE 21

hooked in straight rows or by using the technique of filling (see page 118). The border may be set off from the background by one row in a contrasting color repeated from the pattern. The row along the outer edge or binding may be of yet another color, again repeated from the pattern. These two different colors should be similar in value to the color that predominates in the border, so that all are of equal intensity. A medium blue could be used between a light brown border and a beige background, with a soft red at the outer edge of the rug.

Many rugs have what is known as a dust edge, an innovation of early-day rugmakers. (It is illustrated in Fig. No. 21.) Their ubiquitous dark garments,

121

when discarded, often became backgrounds of rugs. But in a period devoid of electric vacuum cleaners, it was not easy to keep these dark rugs tidy and free of dust and lint at the edges. The women cleverly devised a scheme to conceal the dust—and also their poor housekeeping! They began to make narrow borders a little lighter than the backgrounds of their rugs, so that dust and lint at the edges weren't obvious. The border was drawn with a softly waved line, instead of a straight one. The first row, next to the background, was almost the same color; the hue became gradually lighter toward the outer edge.

Today, even though cleaning is not a problem, the dust edge is a popular kind of border for hooked rugs. It is a mere hint of border in a lighter or darker value of the background color. A rug with a black background may have a dark gray or dark khaki dust border. If you like, a dust edge may be also used with a light background, shading it from light to dark at the outer edge. Any narrow border can be shaped with a waved line, of course, instead of a straight one.

A wide border may be three to six inches in width, consisting of row after row of straight hooking in either horizontal or vertical lines. (See Figs. 22 and 23.) A wide border, hooked horizontally, is more interesting when broken into an uneven number of bands of color in random widths. The wider the border, the wider the bands. Repeat colors from the pattern in different values and combine them with grays, khakis, browns, and beige, with gradual changes from light to dark. Here are examples of two borders in horizontal stripes, showing how to combine colors, values, and textures in wide borders:

(1) *Five-inch border* on rug with beige background and design of golds, reds, and blues. Working inward from outer edge next to binding,

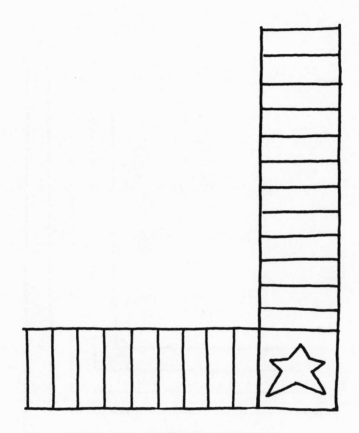

FIGURE 22

mottled dark red band (3 rows black-red-gray plaid)
dark khaki band (2 rows solid color smooth texture)
dark blue band (2 rows tweed)
dark red band (3 rows smooth texture)
dark gray band (3 rows tweed)
medium red band (2 rows solid color smooth texture)
medium gray band (2 rows tweed)
medium khaki band (2 rows tweed)
1 row medium blue between border and background

123

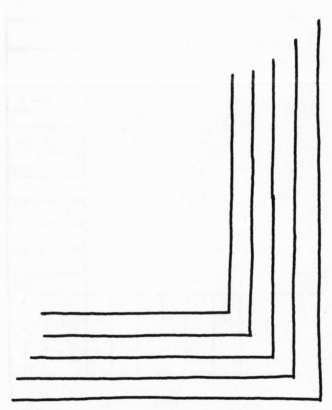

FIGURE 23

(2) *Three-inch border* for rug with gray-blue background and design of reds and khakis. Working inward from outer edge next to binding,

> charcoal brown band (2 rows dark brown, 1 row medium brown)
> dark khaki band (3 rows tweed, 1 row smooth texture)
> muted red band (2 rows mottled red tweed, 1 row lighter red)
> medium brown band (2 rows medium brown smooth texture, 1 row lighter brown tweed)

124

A diagonally striped border is featured in Figure No. 24. A border, four to six inches wide, may be hooked in a diagonal pattern, repeating colors from the design in a variety of values and textures. First, hook one or two straight rows between border and background and one or two straight rows next to

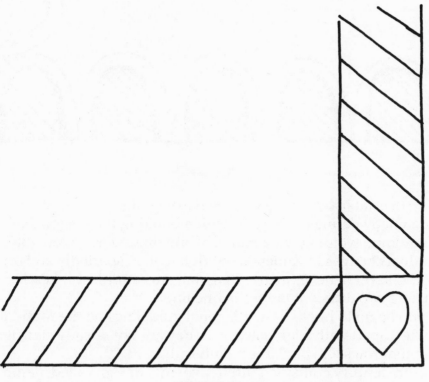

FIGURE 24

125

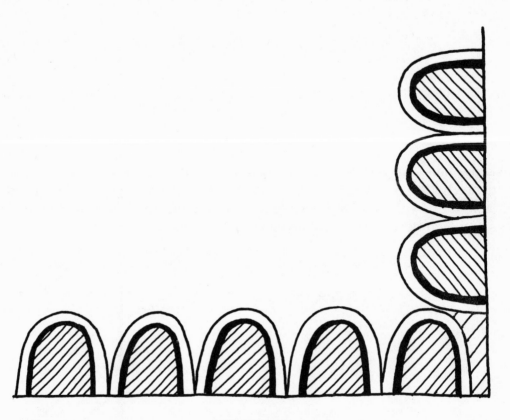

FIGURE 25

the binding to establish the edges of the border. Choose a color for these lines that will distinctly define the border. When hooking the diagonal lines, select colors at random, avoiding wide bands of any one color. Follow the general rule of gradual changes in values. Use bright colors sparingly and only as accents, spaced several inches apart. Diagonal lines may be broken here and there by using two different fabrics in one line.

Before you begin to hook, draw diagonal guidelines on the foundation several inches apart with a felt marker, if they are not already stenciled on the pattern, so that rows will be slanted uniformly.

Nineteenth-century craftsmen often favored a design called "lamb's tongue," which makes a handsome border (see Fig. 25). It features one or

126

more rows of "tongues," their sides butted against each other. Outline each tongue with two or three rows (depending on size of tongues) of contrasting fabrics. Colors and/or values may differ in the separate rows of outlining. Use the technique of "filling," without direction, for center portions of tongues. (This is the shaded area in the drawing.) Fill with the color you choose to predominate in the border, selecting different, yet similar, values and textures at random for more interest.

A modified version of the lamb's tongue is the clamshell design, in which loops are more shallow, each giving the effect of a clamshell, instead of a tongue.

CHAPTER 12

Final Steps and the Care of Finished Rugs

No matter how many rugs you make, you will always feel a tingle of excitement whenever the last loop is hooked and a rug is ready to be removed from the frame.

Just before removing a rug from the frame, check the underneath side for any loose ends that should be pulled through and also for large gaps in hooking. Patches of unfilled foundation can't always be seen from the right side, so mark them by inserting toothpicks through the foundation to the right side, taking care not to split fibers. Fill any open spaces on the right side that are large enough to push your finger into. (See page 66 for advice on very small gaps.) Spotting gaps is always eagerly awaited by the two young sons of one avid rugmaker. They delight in crawling under the frame to locate open patches and poke the toothpicks through.

Now is the time to refer to page 42 for complete directions on how to hem the foundation and sew the binding in place.

Your new rug will look its best after it is steam-pressed. Though you may use a steam iron, pressing first on one side and then on the other, you can give the rug a more thorough steaming by covering it with a wet cotton terry cloth towel that has been wrung out. Using a dry iron, instead of a steam iron, press the wrong side first and then the right side. Make sure that the binding is well pressed so that the rug will lie flat. The rug should remain flat till dry.

A pad under any rug will extend its life and also make it softer underfoot. Rubber padding is best for area rugs, because it helps to prevent skidding and makes them safer to walk on. Never use a rubberized spray on hooked rugs.

Rubber padding in thirty-two and thirty-six-inch widths is inexpensive and can usually be purchased by the yard wherever carpeting is sold. It can be easily cut with scissors to the shape of your rug. It should be one-half-inch smaller than the rug on all sides, so that it will not show at the edges. If padding does not come wide enough for your rug, tape two strips together with wide, adhesive cloth tape. Any good padding made for broadloom rugs is suitable for room-size hooked rugs.

The Care of Hooked Rugs

Once your rug is finally placed on the floor, enjoy it. The more it is walked on, the prettier it will become, as loops meld together with wear and colors soften.

Rugs always last longer if kept clean. Hooked rugs may be cleaned with tank-type electric vacuum cleaners, using the rug nozzles. Area rugs should be cleaned on both sides. Do not shake hooked rugs to free them of dust—this weakens them. They may be commercially cleaned when badly soiled, however. But the less often they are dunked in harsh chemicals, the better.

If you live in the snow belt, you will find that nature provides the best cleaning fluid of all. There's nothing like a bath of clean, dry, powdered snow—the kind skiers love—to refresh hooked rugs. Though this may sound like a figment of somebody's imagination, it really works, because snow consists of pure, soft water, free of harmful chemicals. Lay your rugs outside, sprinkle them with a generous coating of snow, then brush it off with a clean broom. Spread rugs on papers indoors and away from direct heat for drying. Do not lay them on wood floors while still wet.(Moisture damages wood floors.)

Occasionally, on a damp, foggy day, give rugs with burlap foundations an airing out-of-doors in a sheltered place. This will restore moisture to the burlap and prevent it from drying and becoming brittle.

When you roll a rug for storing or transporting it, always roll it with right side to the outside to avoid stretching fibers of the foundation. Never fold a rug. If a rug is to be stored for any length of time, sprinkle a few moth balls or crystals over it before rolling. Wrap it in heavy brown paper or plastic. But do not leave a plastic-wrapped rug in the sun; moisture sometimes forms inside the plastic and causes mildew.

Repairing Hooked Rugs

If the family dog or cat should pull out a few loops in your rug, just hook the wool strip into the same openings as before. If the wool is damaged, it can be replaced by a new strip, as long as the foundation is intact.

An accidental tear in an otherwise sound foundation can be repaired by covering the torn area with monk's cloth, the best material for this purpose even on a burlap foundation. First, rip out the wool loops an inch beyond the hole. Cut the monk's cloth a little larger than the hole to be covered. It is unnecessary to turn under the raw edges of the patch; but, if you wish, you may first finish it with zigzag stitching on a sewing machine. Sew the monk's cloth patch securely, by hand, to the foundation on the underneath side of the rug. Use heavy-duty thread, the color of the wool in the area you are patching, just in case it should show on the right side. Turn the rug to the right side and sew the frayed edges of the old foundation to the patch. Rehook the area, using the same wool that you ripped out, if it is in good condition. If it is not, replace the damaged strips with matching wool.

When a rug acquires a number of breaks from age, a new backing is required. Cut the monk's cloth the shape of the rug, adding enough at the edges to turn under. Sew it to the binding on the underneath side of the rug. Tack it to the old foundation at various places throughout the rug to hold the two backings together. Make small stitches, and try to keep them from showing on the right side. Wherever there is a break in the old foundation, rip out the wool loops around it, about an inch beyond the hole, so that you can sew the frayed edges to the new backing, following directions above for repairing.

A *badly* worn rug probably has frayed edges and needs a new binding, as well as a new foundation. If so, carefully remove the entire binding, and rip out wool loops an inch beyond the edges of the rug. Lay the rug over a piece of monk's cloth and cut the monk's cloth two inches larger than the rug. Sew the new foundation to the underneath side, along all edges of the rug. Then, working from the right side, sew frayed edges, wherever there are breaks, to the new foundation. To bind again, sew new tape to the new foundation, and rehook edges where you ripped out wool. If you cannot match the color of the border, select a contrasting color that blends well. If other areas are wearing thin, it's wise to repair them at this time to preserve your rug.

When a rug has only minor damage at the edges and the tape is intact, simply rip out stitches holding the binding, so that you can repair underneath it, making the kind of monk's cloth patch described above and rehooking where necessary. Sew the original binding back in place.

If a rug is badly worn along the edges from age (edges usually wear out first), yet is in good condition everywhere else, you can add a new binding

131

over the old one. Lay two-inch-wide cotton tape or a wool bias binding, as near the color of the border as possible, along the edge on the right side of the rug. If you can't match the border, select binding in a color that blends, to suggest a narrow border. Sew the new binding to the rug through the wool loops on the right side, at least one-fourth-inch back from the edge. This is about two rows in from the edge of the rug. Overcasting with strong thread, make stitches close together. When you reach a corner, ease the binding around the corner smoothly. After the binding is sewn around the rug, turn it to the underneath side and sew it in place. When the binding is completed, you will have a bound edging, about one-half-inch wide, exposed on the right side of the rug.

CHAPTER 13

Three Rugs Specially Planned for Beginners

The rugs described in this chapter are planned to help beginners; but experienced rugmakers can also reap the benefits of having color schemes and quantities of wool prescribed for them. Select the pattern you like best as a beginning. Or why not make all three!

The quantities of wool given are those actually used by the persons who hooked these rugs. However, it's wise to allow a little extra, since no two people hook exactly the same.

If you prefer to change the color schemes in any of these rugs, you can easily plan your own by following the suggestions here as a guide for balancing and distributing colors. Quantities of wool would remain the same.

Godey Spray

This pattern of gracefully intertwined scrolls, taken from the *Godey's Lady's Book*, was hooked in two different color combinations to show how different treatments of the same pattern can change the effect. This small rug is easy to make and requires very little material, so it is an unusually good pattern for a beginner.

Red Background
None of the wool in this rug (see Color Plate No. 8) was specially dyed.

Cardinal red background: 11 ounces commercially-dyed wool.

Scrolls: outlined with 2 ounces gray-and-black tweed. A second row of outlining was hooked with 2¼ ounces medium gray. Remainder of scrolls filled, in rows, with 3¼ ounces lighter gray.

Veins of scrolls: 1½ ounces very light gray, almost white. One continuous row that outlines each vein hooked with 2¼ ounces light gray.

Berries: outlined in khaki and filled with one strip of light gold wool, 3½ by 16 inches. Seeds of berries, hooked with scrap of Oxford gray wool. (See page 111 for directions on hooking seeds.)

Stems: small piece of dark brown wool.

Beige Background
This totally different color plan (see Color Plate No. 9) gives you another choice for your rug. All wool was commercially dyed.

Beige background: 11 ounces wool.

Scrolls: outlined with 2 ounces gray-and-black tweed. Second row of outlining was hooked with 2¼ ounces taupe flannel. Remainder of scrolls filled, in rows, with 3¼ ounces beige wool that is a darker value than the background.

Veins: 1½ ounces Egyptian red. One continuous row that outlines each vein was hooked in 2¼ ounces paisley from an old shawl.

Berries: outlined in the paisley with a second row in dark red. Remainder of berries filled with lighter red wool, about 3 by 16 inches. (Red tweed or red plaid could be substituted for paisley.)

Seeds: dark gray.

Stems: dark gray tweed.

Mariner's Star

Wool for the background of this rug (see Color Plate No. 10) was purchased by the yard, but all other fabrics were from sewing scraps and old garments.

Background: 17½ ounces medium-weight off-white wool, dyed with "Favorite Light Background" mixture (see page 89).

Pale coral outline of star: 1 ounce beige herringbone wool, overdyed with terra cotta and apricot, combined.

Rust points of star, rust tails of scrolls, rust outlines of gold scrolls, rust outlines of cherries: 6 ounces rust-color smooth, sheer wool from discarded dress.

Four coral points of star: 1 ounce peach flannel, overdyed with apricot, terra cotta, and Egyptian red, combined.

Four gold points of star: 1 ounce medium-weight light gold tweed, overdyed with old gold.

Gold scrolls, gold outlines of their rust tails, 1 row gold between border and background: 5 ounces light yellow-green-tan plaid, overdyed in old gold. (This was a very coarse fabric and required an unusually large quantity of dye. The fabric you use would probably take less.)

Cherries: ½ ounce old gold flannel.

Dark blue-green leaves: 2 ounces medium gray wool, overdyed with reseda green.

Light olive-green leaves and green border: 5 ounces olive-green tweed.

Veins of leaves: small scrap of dark olive-green wool.

Stems: ½ ounce brown-olive-green tweed.

Two rows outlining center of star: scrap of brown-and-coral tweed.

Center of star: ¼ ounce dark gold, smooth, medium-weight wool.

Flat Rose Diamond

This rug is an example of how you can create a rug that will pass as an antique. The muted colors look mellow and aged, with no great contrast in values. (See Color Plate No. 11.) The advantage of this pattern is that most of it can be made from odds and ends of wool fabrics. The seven ounces required for the diamond-shape background is the most of any one wool that you will need. And even that area can be a combination of textures, dyed to match.

> Diamond background: 7 ounces beige wool from an old shawl, purchased from Mrs. Ralph Burnham, wife of the noted collector (see page 26).

> Flowers: top flower outlined in paisley; end flowers outlined in red-black tweed; inner flowers outlined in dark red. All flowers filled with smooth textures dyed in Egyptian red. Centers are outlined with one row brown wool and filled with dull gold tweeds.

> Leaves: large leaves are divided, with lower halves hooked in green-and-tan checks and upper halves hooked in wools that were originally beige and light gray, overdyed in bronze-green. Veins were hooked in two rows, one paisley and one plain red. The small leaves have veins hooked in one row of paisley and are filled with bronze-green.

> Stems: main stem, two rows black-and-gray tweed. All other stems, one row of the same tweed.

137

Striped corners: the uneven bands of color appear to be hit-or-miss, but they were carefully planned to balance colors. Each band contains three or four rows in different values and textures of one color, with occasional strong lines as accents. Rows are broken, here and there, with new colors or textures introduced partway through a row, instead of always at the beginning, to soften the striped effect. The same arrangement of colors and textures should be carried across to opposite corners, so that the effect is a diamond on an old woven rug.

Border: two rows of green-and-khaki plaid.

CHAPTER 14

A Room-Size Project

A room-size rug doesn't require any more skill than a small rug, but it does require more time, more wool—and a lot more strength to carry it around! If you are an ambitious crafts buff, with big ideas of launching a room-size rug instantly, temper your ambition long enough to make at least one small rug first. Hook an area rug in the same colors you would choose for a room-size rug, so that you can be sure you like the combination. If you are satisfied with the small rug, it's safe to begin a large one. If you are dissatisfied, make another small rug, correcting whatever you disliked in the first one.

While you are making a small rug, you can perfect both your hooking and dyeing. And it will give you time to collect more wool. A mountain of wool is required for a room-size rug. You will find that it greedily gobbles up anything you can feed it—old wool blankets, slacks, skirts, and dresses. The background alone may devour seven or eight coats.

The surest way to provide enough wool for a background or other large areas is to dye it yourself, because you can use assorted fabrics and yet repeat colors. Even when you purchase new wool to fortify your supply, you can overdye it to match wool that you have on hand. And since it is unlikely that you can collect enough of the same texture, it's best to begin with assorted textures—smooth and rough, thick and thin. Study how you can bring in different wools if needed, instead of continually trying to duplicate fabrics that you have on hand. Just as in area rugs, a variety of textures and values will make the background of a room-size rug more interesting. Assorted tweeds can be used, but if the background is tweed, limit the tweeds that you use in the design.

Most room-size rugs have designs that are repeated all the way around the rug, requiring an abundance of matching wool. You can cheat on flowers and

139

leaves by making them different, but borders, scrolls, and geometrics should match throughout a rug.

Estimating Quantity of Wool

Before you begin your rug, take the overall dimensions in square feet. Study the pattern and estimate the per cent of background, design, and border. Divide the total number of square feet by the percentages estimated for the different areas. For example, an eight-by-ten rug has eighty square feet. It may be proportioned in this way: background—forty-five per cent or thirty-six square feet; pattern—forty-five per cent or thirty-six square feet; border—ten per cent or eight square feet. Since every square foot in a rug requires about one-half pound of wool, eighteen pounds would be needed for background, eighteen pounds for pattern, and five pounds for the border. And you should always allow more. Now, do you see why you have to collect a *lot* of wool? And why dyeing is recommended.

You can never be absolutely sure that you have enough wool until you begin to hook. But there is a fail-safe way to learn early in the game whether your wool will last. Divide your supply into four equal parts, and store each part in a separate bag. Hide three bags and use the remaining one-quarter of the wool to hook one-quarter of your rug. When you begin the background, begin at either the center portion or the outer edge and work toward the opposite direction, so that if you need to add wool that is different, you can do so at one of these points, instead of between the two areas.

By the time you have hooked one-quarter of your rug, you will know whether you have enough wool to complete it. Resist any temptation to steal from the other three bags. There is always some way to change course in the beginning, such as adding multiple rows of outlining to large motifs or to the border. But you can't wait till the homestretch to make changes, or one side of the rug will be different from the other side. Of course, additions and substitutions made in the first quarter will have to be made in the remaining three-quarters, so plan accordingly and add the necessary wool to the other three bags.

A Room-Size Pattern in Sections

A room-size pattern on burlap must be hooked in two or three sections, since burlap is available only in narrow widths. The sections are joined together by overlapping the selvage edges and hooking them together. The result is a very large rug that appears to be seamless. If you design and draw your own pattern in sections, be sure that overlapping edges, where sections will be joined, are selvage edges. Designers usually indicate a lap of one inch.

Although monk's cloth, such as Meriwell Rug Backing, comes wide enough to make a fifteen-foot rug without piecing, a rug of such size would become too heavy and cumbersome to handle as it becomes filled with loops. So it is really more practical to make a rug in sections. If you should make a large rug without piecing, plan space in your home or studio where the frame may remain undisturbed as long as the rug is in progress.

Selvage edges, where sections will be seamed, must be protected against stretching while the rug is taut on the frame. Thumbtacks should never be inserted in these edges. To provide a temporary substitute edge for tacking, sew heavy cotton fabric strips, about six inches wide, to every selvage edge that will be joined later. You can use old drapery fabric, dungarees, or whatever you have that is sturdy enough to last without splitting. Old sheeting is not strong enough. The cotton fabric is to be securely sewn about one-half inch from the selvage, by hand or by using the long basting stitch on a machine. Since you will have to rip out the stitching later, do not make a tight, fine stitch. When you tack your pattern to the frame for hooking areas near the selvage, insert the thumbtacks through the cotton fabric, instead of through the edge of the foundation. For hooking other areas, tack the pattern in the usual way. (See page 55.)

Binding Sections of a Room-Size Rug

When a rug is made in sections, the tape binding has to be pieced too. But avoid piecing at seam lines, because this would make the edges lumpy. For a smooth binding, follow the steps outlined here. The directions given are for a rug in three sections, with lap lines on Section 2, but the same procedure would apply to a rug in only two sections by omitting steps for the middle section.

Number the sections 1, 2, and 3, on the margins, so that you will keep them in correct order. Study Figure No. 26 carefully before you begin to bind your rug.

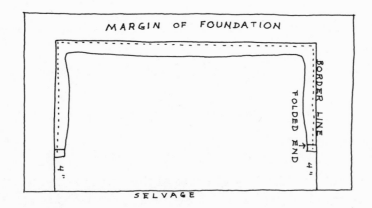

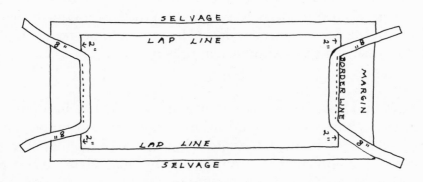

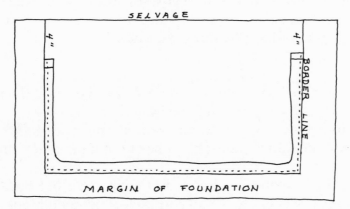

FIGURE 26

Section 1

Sew tape binding to Section 1, beginning at the upper edge, four inches from the selvage edge that is to be joined to Section 2. Fold end of tape back three-fourths-inch and sew tape on three sides of that section, along the outline of the rug (see page 40), until you reach a point on the lower edge of Section 1 four inches from the selvage edge that will be joined to Section 2. Cut tape, leaving three-fourths-inch to fold back at the end.

Section 2

Only the upper and lower edges are bound on Section 2. When you begin to sew the tape to Section 2, leave an additional eight inches of tape at each side, on both upper and lower edges, beyond the points where you begin and end sewing. These extensions will be sewn across the seams later to complete the binding after the rug is hooked. When you sew the tape to Section 2, begin and end sewing two inches from the lap lines at either side, to leave plenty of space for joining and hooking sections together.

Section 3

Bind Section 3 the same as Section 1, beginning and ending the tape four inches from the selvage edge that will be joined to Section 2.

If your rug is in two sections, instead of three, the tape on the second section would be extended an extra eight inches to meet the tape on Section 1.

The extensions of tape on the upper and lower edges of Section 2 are left loose until after the rug is hooked and completely seamed together. See page 147 for directions on joining tape where it is pieced. After all sections are joined, as described below, hem the foundation, turn back the binding and sew it in place, the same as on smaller rugs (see page 42).

How to Hook and Join Sections to Conceal Seams

Seams in a hooked rug can be cleverly concealed if joined correctly, and no one but you will know where they are. Remember that the following directions are for a rug in three sections.

When hooking Sections 1 and 3, leave two or more inches free of loops along the selvages. And leave two inches free on Section 2 along the lap lines (assuming that lap lines are on Section 2). It's really better to leave even more space unhooked on Sections 1 and 3, since they will be on top when lapped. End your hooking unevenly along these lines, because straight lines would make the seams obvious.

Wait to hook any small motifs along seam lines, such as small leaves or flowers, until after you have joined the sections. Set aside a marked bag of wool containing fabrics and colors you will need for these small motifs. Also, set aside enough matching wool to complete any unfinished areas of design and the background along the seams.

To avoid a long row of clipped ends down the seams, which would also make seams obvious, leave long ends of wool dangling underneath, instead of cutting them where you discontinue hooking. Later, after sections are basted together, you can continue hooking across the seams with these same wool strips.

When you are ready to join Sections 1 and 2, remove the cotton fabric sewn to the selvage edges for their protection by carefully pulling out the stitches. Do not stretch the edges of the foundation.

Lay the sections flat on the floor, overlapping edges, as indicated on the pattern, and matching the design. Pin Sections 1 and 2 together the full length of the seam, inserting pins horizontally across the lapped area, one inch apart. This is the area that is not yet filled with loops. When the two sections are completely pinned together, use a felt marker to make one-inch horizontal lines on each section, between and parallel to each pin. These inch-long markings are the lines that you will match when you join the sections permanently.

Measure about sixteen inches in the very center of the lapped seam, and leave pins in this sixteen inches. Remove all other pins.

With a running handstitch and using heavy-duty cotton thread, baste the lapped sections together, along both lapped edges, the length of the sixteen inches that remain pinned. Remove pins after basting. By leaving the edges open above and below the basted area, you will be able to reach underneath the frame with your left hand to hold wool strips as you hook the sections together. (Also, your knees will be between the two sections and you won't have the weight and bulk of a heavy rug on your lap.) If the full length of the seam were basted, it would be impossible to hold the rug in your lap and reach underneath it.

Lay the rug across the frame and tack it, with the basted area in the center of the frame. Hook through the lapped area of foundation, filling it with wool loops to join the sections permanently. Begin hooking with the long ends of wool that you left dangling for this purpose. Hook across the seam in an irregular pattern wherever there is background. Any area of design must be carefully matched as to color and direction of hooking. Use the bag of wool set aside for this purpose.

When you have hooked together the sixteen-inch lapped area, remove the rug from the frame. Match the inch-long markings on the two sections for another sixteen inches, just beyond the area you have hooked together. Again, pin and baste for sixteen inches. Remove pins and follow the steps given above for hooking the sections together.

Continue pinning, basting, and hooking, sixteen inches at a time, until you near the last few inches on that half of the seam. Then, lap the edges, pin, and baste across the borderline of the rug and through the margin. But before returning the rug to the frame for hooking, sew the extension of tape binding on Section 2 across the seam. Follow the outline of the rug, as usual, until the tape meets and laps over the folded end of tape on Section 1. Trim any surplus tape.

Again, tack the rug to the frame and hook the last few inches together on that portion of the seam.

Go back to the center, where you began joining the two sections, and work toward the other end in the same way—pinning, basting, hooking, and joining the tape—until the two sections are completely seamed, hooked, and bound.

Follow all the above directions to join Section 3 to Section 2.

Hem the foundation, turn back the tape, and sew it in place to complete your room-size project.

As soon as your handsome new rug is laid in the room it was made for, why not have a party to display it and to thank the friends who contributed wool? A beautiful conclusion to a long, hard job. And if you're anything like the authors of this book, you enjoyed every minute of it!

A Gallery of Rugs

The following illustrations will provide an additional source of ideas whenever you are choosing patterns. These rugs were hooked by students of Alice Beatty and photographed by her upon their completion in her studio.

LION AND LAMB, Heritage Hill Pattern No. 56A, 27 by 40 inches, hooked by Harry Livermore.

MERRY-GO-ROUND HORSE, original design, hooked by Harry Livermore.

COWARDLY LION, Heritage
Hill Pattern No. 54A, 27 by 40
inches, hooked by Harry Livermore.

PRIMITIVE BIRD, E. Dana Pattern No. 159, 27 by 42 inches.

DUCK DECOY, Heritage Hill
Pattern No. 142, 30 by 42
inches, hooked by Harry Livermore.

STARS AND FLOWERS, E. Dana pattern, hooked by Mary Sargent.

VICTORIAN SCROLL, Heirloom Pattern No. 725C, 30 by 54½ inches, hooked by Mary Sargent.

AUNT MAG'S RUG, Heirloom (Skaket) Pattern No. 99, 34 by 58 inches, hooked by Mary Sargent.

BALTIMORE AND OHIO, E. Dana Pattern No. 1, 24 by 36 inches, hooked by Jean Livermore.

HOMESTEAD, E. Dana Pattern No. 151, 34 by 70 inches, hooked by Mary Sargent.

DRUM, special design by E. Dana, 50-inch round, hooked by Alice Beatty.

MERRY CHRISTMAS, E. Dana
Pattern No. 181, 26 by 40
inches, hooked by Jean Livermore.

BOY FRANKLIN, Craftsman
Pattern No. H200, 37 by 61
inches, hooked by Helen
Nitzsche.

HOUND DOG, Heritage Hill
Pattern No. 16, 18 by 36
inches, hooked by Harry Livermore.

PRIMITIVE OWL, Craftsman Pattern No. H190, 32 by 60 inches.

BIRDS AND BASKET OF FLOWERS, Craftsman Pattern No. H65, 34 by 56 inches.

PRIMITIVE HOUSE, Heirloom Pattern No. 716I, 25 by 46 inches, hooked by Marjorie Grogg.

APPENDIX

Where to Buy Everything for Hooking Primitive Rugs

Only suppliers who sell materials and equipment for hooking primitive rugs are listed here. Dealers who specialize in materials for fine, realistic hooking are not listed, because their patterns, backings, and hooks are not suitable for primitive hooking. If you ask at local craft shops, you will probably find them willing to stock equipment for this kind of hooking if they do not already have it on hand. Take *The Hook Book* with you and show them the supplies needed, such as dyes, hook, and patterns.

Many patterns listed in catalogs are for realistic hooking only, with too many fine details for primitive hooking; so when ordering patterns, ask if they are suitable for primitives. Request that your patterns be stenciled on 8½- or 10-ounce burlap or on monk's cloth. Also, specify that you want only the Susan Bates straight rug hook. Mention *The Hook Book* when writing to suppliers, and they will understand the kind of equipment you need.

When requesting information from suppliers, please enclose a stamped, self-addressed postcard or envelope. Do not send money until you know how much is due.

Here is a list of suppliers from whom you may order by mail:

BERRY'S OF MAINE, 20-22 Main Street, Yarmouth, Maine 04096. Cushing Perfection Dyes and Plurosol, wool by the yard, tape binding, tracing pencils, extra-long thumbtacks. List of rugmaking supplies available.

BRAID-AID FABRICS, 466 Washington Street, Pembroke, Massachusetts 02359. Complete line of supplies for primitive rugs. Fraser frame, Cushing Perfection Dyes and Plurosol, Susan Bates hook, tape binding, wool by the yard, Bliss cutter, extra-long thumbtacks. Patterns: Heritage Hill (order on monk's cloth); Craftsman, including Burnham designs; and Karl Kraft Studio patterns (order on 8½- or 10-ounce burlap). Catalog available.

LIB CALLAWAY PATTERNS, 109 Shady Knoll Lane, New Canaan, Connecticut 06840. Order patterns on 10-ounce burlap. Catalog available.

W. CUSHING & COMPANY (JOAN MOSHIMER), North Street, Kennebunkport, Maine 04046. Fraser frame, Cushing Perfection Dyes and Plurosol, pattern pencils, Susan Bates hooks, wool by the yard, tape binding, Bliss cutters, extra-long thumbtacks. Patterns: Craftsman Hooked Rug Patterns—Burnham designs are designated by the letter H before the number. Order patterns on primitive burlap or monk's cloth. Catalog available and also a dye color card.

THE DORR MILL STORE, Main Street, Guild, New Hampshire 03754. Wool by the yard in wide range of colors. Color card available.

EDANA RUG PATTERNS, 196 West Norwalk Road, Darien, Connecticut 06820. Order patterns on 10-ounce burlap. Catalog available.

HARRY M. FRASER, 192 Hartford Road, Manchester, Connecticut 06040. Patterns, frames, hooks, dyes, monk's cloth.

HEIRLOOM RUGS, 28 Harlem Street, Rumford, Rhode Island 02916. Order patterns on 10-ounce burlap. Catalog available.

HERITAGE HILL PATTERNS, Box 624, Westport, Connecticut 06880. Order patterns on monk's cloth.

KARL KRAFT STUDIO, Severns Bridge Road, South Merrimack, New Hampshire 03083. Order patterns on 10-ounce burlap. Catalog available.

JANE OLSON RUG STUDIO, 4645 West Rosecrans Avenue, Hawthorne, California 90250. Fraser frames, Susan Bates hooks, Dorr woolens, Cushing dyes, and patterns.

PATCHWORK SAMPLER, 9735 Clayton Road, Saint Louis, Missouri 63124. Original patterns, Craftsman patterns, artist available for custom designs, Susan Bates hooks, complete line of Dorr wool, burlap, frames, cutters, and craft books. Inquiries welcomed.

GEORGE WELLS, Cedar Swamp Road, Glen Head, Long Island, New York 11545. Cushing dyes and Plurosol, Susan Bates hooks, extra-long thumbtacks, cotton monk's cloth (Meriwell backing) by the yard, tape binding, George Wells Patterns, stenciled on monk's cloth. Catalog not available.

Index

Beatty